Uncocooned

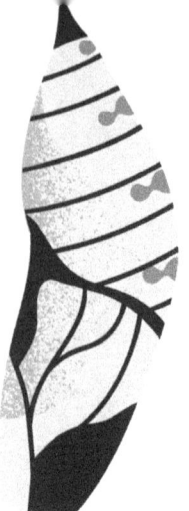

A Memoir of Metamorphosis:

Faith, Resilience, Reinvention,
and the Courage to Begin Again

SHELLY REXROAT

UNCOCOONED

A Memoir of Metamorphosis: Faith, Resilience, Reinvention, and the Courage to Begin Again

Copyright © 2025 by Bethesda Designs, LLC

All rights reserved. No part of this book may be reproduced, distributed, or transmitted in any form or by any means, including photocopying, recording, or other electronic or mechanical methods, without the written permission from the publisher or author, except as permitted by U.S. copyright law or in the case of brief quotations embodied in a book review.

Disclaimer: This book has been published for the purpose of providing the reader with general information on its subject matter. The author and the publisher believe the information to be accurate and authoritative at the time of publication. The book is sold with the understanding that neither the author nor the publisher is providing professional advice, and the reader should not rely upon this book as such. Every situation is different, and professional advice (whether psychological, legal, financial, tax, or otherwise) should only be obtained from a professional licensed in your jurisdiction who has knowledge of the specific facts and circumstances.

Scripture taken from THE HOLY BIBLE, NEW INTERNATIONAL VERSION®, NIV® Copyright © 1973, 1978, 1984, 2011 by Biblica, Inc.® Used by permission. All rights reserved worldwide.

Cover Design by Anton Khodakovsky
Interior Layout and Design by Brittany Becker
Editorial Team: Hallie Knox, Jarah Byron, Becca Blackburn, Rachel Maier

ISBNs:
E-book: 979-8-89165-314-6
Paperback: 979-8-89165-315-3
Hardcover: 979-8-89165-316-0

Published by:
Streamline Books
Kansas City, MO
shareyourstory.com

To my husband, Donnie, who has stood by me through so many seasons with unwavering love—thank you for being my safe place and steady rock. You are truly the one who walks beside me in life's journey.

To my mother, Dayna, and sisters, Tiffany and Stephanie— your faith, strength, and grace taught me what it means to be a woman anchored in God and lifted by love. A bond forged in fire is not easily broken and the resiliency in which each of you have overcome your own challenges is an ongoing inspiration to me.

To my dad, Mike, and sisters, Tandee and Michaele—I'm amazed at the way God restored and knit our families together. And to my extended family on all sides—you are such beautiful threads in the tapestry of my life, and I love you.

To my grandmother and granddad—I am a living legacy of your faith, generosity, consistency, and deep love which provided the air currents lifting me to new heights. Although I miss you deeply, you are still seen in the generations that came after you.

To all the family and friends who have encouraged me, believed in me, and reminded me of who I am when I'd forgotten—this book is for each of you. You've been part of my metamorphosis, helping me emerge from dark places into light, beauty, and flight.

Contents

Introduction ix

Caterpillar xiii
1. Beginnings 1
2. Living in Darkness 11
3. Waking Up and Moving Forward 19

Molting 27
4. When Everything Falls Apart 29
5. A New Season 39
6. Dreams Deferred 43
7. The Entrepreneurial Years 47

Cocoon 53
8. The Eye of the Storm 55
9. Dissolving: The Health Crisis That Changed Everything 67
10. Being Remade 75

Butterfly 85
11. The Messy Process of Breaking Free 87
12. Looking Back, Moving Forward 93

Notes 98
Acknowledgments 101
About the Author 103

Introduction

I'M NOT GOING to open this book with a harrowing scene from my childhood or an inspirational passage from the Bible. Those might be appropriate starting points for the story that's to come—a story of pain and healing, of prayers and miracles, of God's loving constancy in the darkest valleys, of being broken down and remade into the creation He intended me to be. It's a story that I pray will give you hope, encourage you to see opportunities for joy all around you, and remind you of who you really are even in your moments of deepest suffering, confusion, and grief.

But I'm not going to start there.

Instead, I'm going to start with a bug.

Specifically, a butterfly.

Everyone knows the life cycle of a butterfly—egg to hungry caterpillar to cocoon to delicate, iridescent wings—but there's a bit more to it than what you remember from second-grade science class. That stage between creepy-crawly feet and fluttering flight holds something far more disruptive than a cozy, peaceful little nap. In the cocoon, the caterpillar dissolves entirely and turns to goo. And then somehow, within that soupy mess, something sacred happens. New life takes shape.

That's what this book is about: the goo stage.

It's about the moments in life when everything falls apart. When you feel shattered, the diagnosis drops, or the dream disappears, and you're left wondering how anything good could possibly come from this. This book is about loss and brokenness, and those dark nights of the soul when you wonder if God has gone quiet for good.

Even more, it's about the remaking that comes next—the healing and surprises, the prayers that reached heaven and echoed back, the peace that comes when no peace makes sense, the laughter that shakes you instead of tears.

I've lived through my own dissolving, and God is still putting me back together again. This is the story of my uncocooning.

My dad died when I was young. My stepfather was abusive. Our family business was lost in a heartbreaking betrayal. I've faced infertility, surgeries, and a medical crisis that nearly killed me. I've lost pieces of myself and stood in scenes of wreckage time and time again. But I've also seen miracles, laughed in waiting rooms, and been held together by the grace and gentle persistence of a God who has never stopped His work of weaving my broken pieces back together into something whole.

This book is for anyone who has been there too, or who is there right now. You're not alone. You'll make it through. You are not finished. It may just feel like a painful mess now, but God is turning you into a butterfly.

Life in the cocoon can feel so dark, disorienting, confusing, complicated, and uncertain. You've been dissolved, and you no longer feel like the person you used to be. Yet all the pieces that make you you truly are still there—the dreams that died, the talents that went to sleep, the steps you previously took along this winding journey of life. You are just in an intense process of transformation to become who you were designed to be all along by an author and creator who knows the story from start to end!

So, how do you manage life's mess and uncertainties from inside the cocoon, when everything is being fundamentally transformed?

INTRODUCTION

Sometimes it feels like God has reached into a drawer, pulled out a forgotten treasure, wiped off the dust, and begun fitting together all the broken, fractured pieces along with the strong and beautiful ones. You start to see the truth: Every blow the enemy meant to crush you has instead made you stronger—like a sword forged and hammered into shining sharpness.

My hope is that in these pages, you'll find space to breathe and maybe even laugh. Most of all, I pray you'll find glimmers of hope and signs that you're being carried and made new, even now. I truly believe your story isn't over, and that God is actively making something beautiful out of whatever has been broken.

You were created for a higher purpose, and you have been given strength to overcome. There is beauty within you waiting to break forth. May you shine your light, and wherever the light shines, let it drive out the darkness.

PART 1

Caterpillar

CHAPTER 1

Beginnings

DID YOU KNOW that monarch butterflies only lay their eggs on the leaves of the milkweed plant? Maybe you've seen the hardy, sun-loving native wildflowers before—they have thick stems, broad leaves, and clusters of star-shaped flowers that range from pink to orange to white. In the late summer and fall, they form fuzzy seed pods that burst open and send their silk swirling in the breeze. They're lovely, and especially beloved by those equally lovely insects, the monarchs.

Though adult monarch butterflies gather nectar from the wide range of God's sweet flowers, monarch caterpillars exclusively eat milkweed leaves. The smooth green surface where they were placed by their parent turns out, also, to provide the only sustenance the caterpillars will ever need—besides, that is, their own nutrient-rich eggshells, which they turn back to devour immediately after hatching. I can't help but feel a little whimsical when I picture it and imagine them whispering a thank you to the thing that formed them as they begin to nibble. And then they move on to the milkweed leaves—the only home and the only nourishment they'll know before they get their wings—and start growing.

The funny thing is that milkweed leaves are toxic to most creatures, and when the caterpillars eat them, they're not only fortified but also given a sort of chemical armor against predators. That's the dream, isn't it? A life that begins with abundance, sustenance, and a hardy protection against the dangers to come. A beginning that nourishes and defends. I'd pray we humans could all have such a full start in life, in the form of a warm home and loving family to give us strength! In so many ways, that's how it was for me—and thank God. I certainly needed that nourishment and those tools in order to grow, to begin being drawn together into who God made me to be, and to prepare for the storms to come.

I'll begin at my beginning.

My parents met and were married on Christmas Day in their hometown of Clovis, New Mexico, when my father was twenty-two and my mom was fresh out of high school. She'd been raised in a family that valued independence and operated in quiet defiance and dismissal of constrained male and female stereotypes, by parents who encouraged her to do whatever she set her mind to—so my grandparents were a bit beside themselves when, out of the wide myriad of the world's possibilities, their daughter chose to set her mind to marriage at the ripe old age of eighteen! My granddad insisted that she get a college degree no matter what and sent the new couple off to Memphis to make it happen. My father attended dental school there, too, stepping into his new family's inherited tradition (both my granddad and great-grandfather on my mother's side were also, coincidentally, dentists). Then they returned to Clovis, eventually buying a house just one block away from my mother's parents. What a blessing that turned out to be.

We lived on the edge of Clovis, right where the town road turned into a country highway. Our house had a long driveway and a red tile roof, with three distinctive arches out front that made it easy to spot.

There was a big open patio above the garage; a door from my room opened right onto it. The backyard was wide and sunny, and though we never had horses (my older sister is severely allergic to anything equine), we had space for them. We were close enough to the grade school to walk there alone each day, and we took our time as we went, because our path meandered through an entrancing field of sunflowers. I remember picking ladybugs off the golden petals and gently lifting horny toads to perch on the palms of my hands with their soft underbellies, exhilarated by the freedom and responsibility of that adult-free walk, never knowing my mother could see us from an upstairs window the whole time. She was a magician at striking that balance, giving us our independence without taking her loving, watchful eye off of us (just as, I believe, God does). She had been a wild, determined child herself. She insisted on making a birthday cake without help at the age of five and catapulted herself off the roof with a friend as a young child, so she knew from experience that we children needed a healthy combination of both freedom and guidance!

Inside our home, there was music—always music. My mom played piano, and sometimes the organ, even floating around from church to church to provide accompaniment as needed, organ playing being such a rare skill. The grand piano stood in the formal living room, where we'd often make up little plays on the fireplace hearth and put on performances with our small tambourines and shakers. It was a house full of melodies and laughter, where we children felt safe and loved, as independent and supported and carefree as could be.

But I'm getting ahead of myself.

Early in their marriage, my parents struggled unsuccessfully to get pregnant. Eventually they adopted my oldest sister, but it was almost as if God had simply paused their ability to conceive for a while in order to make sure she was placed in our family, because about a year later I was born. My younger sister came along shortly after that. When we were young, the three of us were blessed to have a stay-at-home mother (college educated, though—Granddad made darn sure of that!), and Dad worked away in his own dental practice.

My childhood wasn't all sunshine and roses, I suppose. In fact, I think it's a wonder that my mom survived my first few years—at the time, she probably thought it a wonder that I did. I was a very sick baby, and troublesome to boot. Having been born breech, I began rolling over almost immediately upon coming home from the hospital (and was climbing out of my crib by eight months, perhaps emulating my feisty, roof-jumping mother). I didn't sleep more than a few hours each day in those first months, crying incessantly instead, ending up in the hospital with IVs in my head and ankle to provide the sustenance that bottles weren't able to provide. It is a small miracle that I survived. It hurts my heart now to think about how my mom must have felt back then, watching her baby's belly swell from malnutrition even though she was trying so hard to nourish me. The noise and worry frazzled her last nerve, but she still had the wherewithal to take me to an old-school country doctor who suggested that I might be allergic to milk and put me on a Jello water diet, which brought such instant and immediate relief for both of us. Sounds odd now, but my food for the first few years consisted of Jello water, bananas, and oatmeal. It was no milkweed leaf, but my health and energy improved… and that brought challenges of its own.

I was a strong-willed and emotional child, with very high highs and very low lows. As I've said, I come from a long line of strong-minded women, and my grandparents' values of independence and stick-to-itiveness showed up in me with full force! By age three, my refusal to let anybody tie my shoes required tremendous patience: I insisted I could "do it myself," constantly making the whole family run late to wherever we were going. Luckily for all of us, my mom—who, again, had been a fierce and forceful child herself and understood the experience from within—steadily and graciously helped me to redirect that stubborn, rebellious energy into a quiet grit that would allow me to persevere through the difficulties of life to come.

Those early health struggles didn't exactly disappear under the pure force of my will, however. They were just the beginning. As an adult, I found myself facing infertility and undertook all sorts of diagnostic testing throughout that long journey. After years of testing, poking, and prodding, I went to a functional medicine center—and the food allergies came full circle. Turns out, I was still allergic to dairy, as well as eggs and gluten! But we didn't know that when I was young.

At such a young age, Mom didn't realize that my food allergies somehow affected my ears and hearing, either. My ears would fill with fluid, causing temporary (but frustrating) hearing loss. There were times I functioned basically like a normal toddler, and other times I would struggle to communicate and just fly into a rage, a bit like Helen Keller. Mom was baffled. She finally figured it out one day when I was on my tricycle and she called out, "Let's go!" (normally my very favorite thing to hear!), and I didn't even flinch. That moment of realization led to ear tubes, which helped tremendously. I became almost an entirely different child overnight, and that experience has shaped my relationship with communication—and my empathy for those who struggle to communicate—ever since.

As I look back at those early years, I can see how the challenges and blessings together prepared me to become who I am today. I wonder if you can say the same. When you reflect on your early years, can you place a finger on the golden moments, the precious gifts… and the darkness and struggles, as well? I wonder how those formative experiences continue to show up for you today. I trust that God's hand was at work, even then, carefully preparing you for the ups and downs of your life to come. I challenge you to spend some time remembering, and finding the ways the work had already begun, and thinking about what that might mean for you now as you navigate both joys and sorrows alike.

My early experiences, both negative and positive, certainly combined with God's gifts for me and began to shape me just as I needed to be shaped. I tended to be a very methodical, thoughtful child, asking "Why?" about absolutely everything. I took everything seriously, which made it difficult for me to understand jokes or even figures of speech. When my mom said to jump into the car, I literally hopped.

This tendency toward literalism was oddly upended in a terrible, pivotal moment when I was five.

We all went to bed as usual, but in the morning woke to life-changing news. I was told—gently and kindly, I'm sure, by my mom's best friend—that my father had passed away during the night, and I had the most peculiar reaction. I laughed and laughed, saying it was the funniest joke I had ever heard. Truly, I believe that laughter was a gift God planted in me to help soften the rough and hard places in life. I'm not saying I recommend treating life's hardest moments as jokes, like I accidentally did during that horrible conversation as a child. But from that moment on, through every trial I faced, laughter would bubble up in the most unlikely moments and cushion the hardest blows, allowing me to move forward with hope and grace.

I pray you find the gift of joy throughout your darkest moments, too. God's laughter has traced my life with gold, and I don't know how I could have gotten through without it.

The previous night, my parents had gone to sleep as usual, my older sister crawling into bed with them as she often did. When my mom first felt my dad begin to jerk beside her, she thought he was just playing around. Soon, however, it became all too clear that something serious was happening. My father was having a heart attack.

Mom quickly started CPR and, in between pumps, got my sister out of the room, called 911, and went downstairs to unlock the front door—surely a feat of adrenaline. We lived on the outskirts of town, as I've said, and had no nearby streetlights. The ambulance driver couldn't seem to locate the house properly in the dark, delaying the arrival of help for far too long. The treatments for cardiovascular events then were also not as advanced as they are currently. They were unable to save him.

That left my mom a widow in her thirties, with three young daughters all under the age of seven. Our lives would never be the same.

Have you ever lost someone you love? I've heard it said that all griefs and losses—like all souls and all relationships—are as different from one another as fingerprints or snowflakes, and of course that's true. But I've also found there's often a strange solidarity amongst those who have been bereaved, whether they lost a loved one as a child or an adult, to disease, accident, or suicide, while close together or far apart. If your heart has walked that desert of grief, I want you to know how sorry I am. I want you to know that God weeps with you, and that Jesus once spoke these words: "Blessed are those who mourn, for they will be comforted."[1]

One of the main things I remember from that difficult time is how our St. Bernard dog, Napoleon, became a protector of the family. He must have sensed our pain and vulnerability, though I can't be sure. My grandparents came by often to watch over us and to help. When my granddad would play and tickle us, our squeals would compel Napoleon to come stand between us girls and our granddad, ready to protect us. Though he was such a large dog, he started to be able to walk so quietly down the stairs that you wouldn't even realize he had come to check things out until you saw him standing there, faithful and alert. He was like a guardian angel of sorts, and I thank God for his warm presence.

It's funny, the weird, blurred way you remember things from such a young age. My younger sister had it even harder than me. Having lost him at the age of three, she quickly found she couldn't recall my dad at all. But what stood out in my memories were the little things: like my dad's watch and belt buckle that had turquoise in them. And the little coffee straws, sugar cubes, and plastic coffee cup holders at the small local airport where my dad had a plane. And then, when he would fly us around at night, how the lights of a nearby city looked from the

---

1. Matthew 5:4

sky. Years later I could still feel and hear the swooshing sound of his heartbeat and breathing when I was lying against his chest, in a way that probably would not have been imprinted on my mind with such strength without the stamp of loss and grief. Odd, how those sharpest and most painful emotions can allow us to hold on to our brightest, most beautiful memories.

Thankfully, we weren't alone in the aftermath of my father's passing. The strong bonds within our family provided an example of God's love in the midst of turmoil and allowed us to weather the storm, knowing God was present, carrying us through using our very love for one another. My grandparents—especially my mom's parents—were beacons of faith and love. They had served as missionaries in Honduras, Kenya, and the Bahamas, were pillars of the community and of our local church, and modeled generosity as a way of life. My granddad had lost his own father during the flu pandemic of 1918, when he was just three, so he understood what it meant to lose a parent young, and he faithfully encouraged us girls—just as he had encouraged our mother—to strive hard and reach high.

The steady presence of my grandparents just down the street made all the difference, especially during that time. We spent so many hours at their house, which was surrounded by an abundance of apple trees and gooseberry bushes, with a little hand-built waterfall and rock pool, and a wide field that their bull would so often escape from, running down the alley to a chorus of shouts from the Italian neighbors. When we visited them, we would walk down the long driveway and past the big window behind a verbena "snowball" bush where we almost always saw our grandparents waiting for us, their faces lighting up at the sight of our approach. We were nourished by their love, their faith, and their Southern-hospitality-influenced cooking—around a properly set table, of course, with linens and fancy dishes. Their chicken and homemade noodles for Sunday dinner after church was my favorite. And their influence gave me a foundation I would come to lean on throughout life.

Prayers began each meal, and stories told around the table were filled with laughter, gratitude, inspiration, adventure, wisdom, and questions of thoughtful intellect. On special occasions, they would do a "taffy pull," from a guarded secret recipe, using a hay hook that was situated in the doorway between the kitchen and dining room. (That activity now reminds me of the way God sometimes pulls, stretches, and twists us, making us stronger and sweeter in that process.) My grandparents taught me that hardship doesn't have to harden you, and generosity is about how you show up for others—over and over—with whatever you have.

We all spend the first few years of our lives deeply learning, whether we remember it or not. I wonder what you may have learned, and how it brought you to where you are now.

Looking back now, I can see how the themes of my early life became the roots of everything that followed. I was and still am that intense little girl, asking too many questions, taking things a bit too seriously, tying her own shoes far too slowly, and learning—sometimes through pain, sometimes through God's gift of laughter—what it means to keep going.

CHAPTER 2

Living in Darkness

HOW LONG DOES a caterpillar remain a caterpillar? I'm not sure—my guess is, not that long. But I bet it feels long, to them. As they seek out leaves to chomp on, dodging predators and the eager, bruising hands of children, do their numbered days seem to drag along, interminable and dream-like—the way I remember my own childhood? Is that how you remember yours?

I was so little when my dad died, and so little when my mom met the man who would quickly become my stepfather. They were married within two years of my dad's death; he formally adopted us when I was eight, erasing my father's last name with his own.

I believe he saw my mother as easy prey: widowed young, with three little girls to provide for, and well-to-do (thanks to my father's life insurance, their dental practice ownership, and their co-ownership with a friend in an airport fixed-base operation). She was vulnerable, and he was predatory in a snake oil salesman kind of way—smooth and charming on the outside and brutally mean behind closed doors. My mother knew she was in terrible trouble before the honeymoon had even ended, but she already saw herself as hopelessly trapped. She had been taught that marriage was forever. She was afraid of him—with his unpredictable cruelty—and ashamed of herself for not having seen through his act. So what else was she supposed to do but deal with the choice that had been made?

He was quite a bit older than her, had already been married twice before, and had three grown sons. Two of his sons lived with him after their parents' divorce; the third, who was raised in his mother's home instead, turned out far healthier and more grounded than his brothers. He would later tell my mom that the man once grabbed him and beat his head against the bathroom mirror for putting too much toothpaste on his toothbrush. My stepfather's ex-wife, too, would eventually tell my mother about the time he threw a fishhook at her simply because she asked him not to leave her to go fishing on her birthday—embedding the hook deeply in her face. There were many such stories, all coming too late to be anything but confirmation for us.

We never knew what would trigger his anger or who his scapegoat would be. It could happen in the middle of a perfectly pleasant dinner, out of the thin blue air, and he might direct the rage at any one of us. In spite of how causeless and random it always was, he was a master at making you feel like it was all your fault—like you deserved it—that he was the righteous and put-upon spiritual leader of the family, being forced into ugliness by our misbehavior.

I remember the first time he hurt me. I was six or seven, and it was not long after the wedding. My sisters and I were taking a bath together when the other two began to squabble about something or other, and I think it was irritation over the clamor that set him off. He burst into the room and yanked me up, naked and dripping wet as I was, then started beating me hard enough to leave bruises all over.

My mom was so furious that I actually thought she might kill him. They had a huge fight. The result was that, from then on, he never left bruises. Oh, he'd twist our arms till it felt like they might break, but he never left a mark. And as far as I know, he never laid a violent hand on my mother. Maybe her reaction to my beating warned him that doing so might push her over the edge. Instead, he stuck to insulting, manipulating, and belittling her.

Life was such a strange, fragmented thing back then. Inside the home, we lived in fear. But outside was the wide, shining world, and there were still so many good things. We girls were deeply involved in our church, took roles in musicals, built friendships at school, joined sports teams, learned to dance, and to play different instruments. We kept things compartmentalized. We didn't bring the darkness and secret shames of home into the shiny outside world. If you've experienced domestic abuse yourself, I wonder if this sounds familiar. And if you're experiencing it right now, I want to tell you: You're not alone. There is light to be found, but it begins with letting that secret darkness out into the open, where God can begin the work of healing. It begins with talking to someone. You don't have to be trapped. You can break free. There are resources out there. And if you don't believe me as you read these words—because you can't pay the bills on your own if you escape, you worry you won't be believed, or you fear for your safety—I am begging you to take a look at the list of organizations and resources included on my website, uncocooned.com/get-help (for easy access, scan the QR code on this page). There are people and programs out there that can help you. You are not alone.

I don't think anyone ever told me anything like that when we were in the midst of the abuse, simply because we hid the situation so well that no one really knew! Personally, I found the most protection in invisibility. Or rather, as a naturally shy and introverted child, my preexisting talent for invisibility proved to have protective benefits—leading me to become entirely too dependent on the safety of my own shell (something God would later confront me about and intentionally unravel in my adulthood). We all avoided my stepfather's unpredictable rage and emotional abuse by "walking on eggshells," as my mother often called it. This meant never expressing negative emotions, "being tough" (so you would never cry, for example), wearing a mask of pretending everything was okay all the time, and reading every detail of people and situations in ways that were imperceptible to others. He was like a raging alcoholic without the alcohol. At least if it had stemmed from a drinking problem, we could have seen the triggers. But it wasn't. So I developed the skill of sensing any possible change in mood or energy in the room, shifting quickly from normal joy or laughter immediately into speaking little, avoiding eye contact, and slipping out like a ghost before his gaze could settle on me.

My older sister, who also dealt with math-related learning disabilities, a condition that caused her to easily get blisters, a lazy eye, and the emergence of epilepsy during this time, taught me to never give up. Whereas almost everything came naturally and easily to me—especially math—almost everything was difficult for her. Rather than make excuses or lower the standards, my mom and grandparents spent hours working with her to learn and overcome, doing things like putting a patch over her good eye and making her use the lazy eye to color in any O's or zeros in a newspaper until her lazy eye got as strong as the other one. They saw the potential in her to be just as good at things as anybody else. Watching their patience, persistence, and optimism with her helped me develop an extraordinary amount of patience as well, and I watched with growing awe for her resilience and positive attitude while overcoming challenges. After all, if she could soldier on so patiently in spite of all her roadblocks—even as a child, even in the midst of our shared, traumatic home life—how could I do anything less?

Our younger sister's form of "soldiering on" during the abuse of this period had a slightly bolder flavor. She wasn't one to take abuse lying down and often pushed back against our stepfather in ways that made me nervous. I even remember her throwing a fishing reel into the lake to put an end to one unbearable fishing trip, then looking him dead in the eyes and saying, "I was eating a peach, and it slipped right out of my hands!"

My mother, for her part, fell into the coping mechanism she'd seen modelled by her parents: stoicism and good old "muscling through." Whether it was because of feelings of shame or her inherited stubbornness, she simply didn't talk about what was happening to anyone, determined to get her family through it on her own. In fact, I'm quite sure my grandparents themselves didn't know anywhere near the half of it. I wonder if they'd have done something about it if they had.

Around this same time, something happened that would transform my family permanently: My mother began to build a business.

My mom had a friend who was also in an abusive marriage. At one point, the friend's husband kicked her out, forcing her to make her own way in the world without a job or experience. So my mom said she would be happy to help her. Together, they would start a business. They say that entrepreneurs build their businesses out of inspiration or desperation, and my mom's friend certainly fell into the latter camp.

They both had backgrounds in music and art and decided to start with music songwriting first. In 1984, they headed off to the Christian Music Artist Seminar in Estes Park, Colorado. My mom left us with my uncle and his family for most of the conference, except for the final concert at the end. Musicians such as Michael W. Smith, Amy Grant, Lisa Whelchel, Larnelle Harris, and Sandi Patty were there. But I was most enamored with a punk rock singer from Scotland whose act included a smoke machine and an over-the-top flair for the dramatic. That sparked my love for music, performing, drama, and poetry—with a sense of adventure that inspired me. Her name was Sheila Walsh.

After returning, it became clear that it made more sense for the aspiring business partners to pursue art instead of music. They decided that creating artwork featuring Scripture verses in calligraphy and watercolor might be a better option. However, neither knew how to do either! So, my mom learned calligraphy while her friend learned watercolor. She ultimately returned to her husband, and they began working out of the friend's garage. The product line they developed together was originally called Sweet Communion, and the business—eventually named The Vineyard—shaped my entire life in huge ways. But there will be much more on that later.

My whole childhood with that man in our house is a sort of bleary, nightmarish blur when I look back on it, with very few events solidly anchored in time. My stepfather didn't contribute financially to the household and would rage and rail if asked to do so, pointing a finger until my mother felt small and crazy. I'm sure that the financial instability and the feeling of being trapped were at least part of the reason my mother ultimately became an entrepreneur: in order to build us an exit strategy.

Her first attempt at escape didn't stick, however; my mother and stepfather separated briefly when I was in ninth grade, and there was a quick breath of healing and light before she took him back again. It was so bewildering and heart-wrenching to experience the end of that short-lived reprieve, and his return left me feeling beyond hopeless.

At the time, I found my mother's choice to allow him back into our lives completely baffling, but I've learned some things since then. The painful, broken experience of an abusive relationship has such a strange gravitational pull that once it ends, your entire comfort zone feels unhinged and broken. It almost feels foreign and somehow wrong to move through the world without its shadow hanging over you. It's easy to find yourself running back into your abuser's arms.

If you're in the midst of extricating yourself from an abusive situation, fighting your own strange urge to return, I hope you hear me when I say this: You can't "get out" halfway. You can't break free unless you go through that awkward, painful reorientation. Don't cling to what you know is sick. Work through the part of you that's still whispering, "It's my fault, not theirs," or "They could still change!" You can't save or heal or change them. You have to break free.

But that time, at least, my mother did not break free—and it was one of the darkest periods of my life. I do remember, even in the depths of that despair, that there was a moment when God made Himself very, very present to me. He reminded me that all feelings—from the tears of a child who has scraped their knee to the very hopelessness I was engulfed in—are only ever temporary. On the other side of the shadow is the light. On the other side of anguish is hope. You have to recognize your feelings and not give into them. Even when you forget what it's like to feel normal, when it seems you've been underwater for a lifetime, you have to remind yourself that it won't last—and that good things are just around the corner.

When have you been in the depths of darkness, unable to believe the pain might ever end? Oh, there are so many things that can set you down (and keep you down) in the sticky, hope-sucking cradle of depression in this brokenhearted world: addiction, poverty, homelessness, human trafficking, abuse, bullying, the foster care system, you name it. Whatever has brought you low and into the darkness, my heart goes out to you.

By the way, there are no small or large traumas, in my opinion—all our pains, whatever they may be, play a role in forming us. Maybe it isn't even your own suffering on your mind today, but the suffering of someone you love—someone you are watching from the outside, standing ready to help while feeling utterly helpless. Perhaps, like me and so many of us, your own suffering has to do with your father. If that's you, I'll remind you of what brought me great comfort during this time: We have a perfect Father in God, and He can give us what no earthly father ever could.

Whatever your situation, I truly believe that God can bring miraculous breakthroughs, and that prayer is often the strongest tool we have. I can also testify that throughout the course of my life, God has worked His way through all the broken pieces of me that ever needed healing, weaving them back together for good—dissolving and reassembling me like a butterfly forming in the cocoon… but we'll get to that.

My main point is this: Have faith. Someday, somehow, God will redeem even the most shattered parts of you in the most unexpected of ways. You're not crazy, or weak, or alone, and God will surround you with people who can strengthen you as you move forward. Trust in Him, and trust that healing is possible. I pray you'll cling to that hope, even as you walk through this valley.

Somewhere around my junior year in high school, my mother and my stepfather finally, truly ended things. Mom wanted to get him out of our lives with such fierce urgency by then that she was willing to give him whatever he wanted during the divorce proceedings. He wound up with many of our household items, including my father's treasured collection of antique guns—but it didn't matter. He was gone.

CHAPTER 3

Waking Up and Moving Forward

M**Y STEPFATHER DID** make a few weak attempts to stay involved in our lives after the divorce, but eventually my younger sister wrote him a letter asking him to leave us in peace. All three of us signed our names like we were filing an ultimatum—on the order of Martin Luther nailing his Ninety-Five Theses to the Wittenberg church door—a bold public declaration of revolution and freedom.

My healing process felt an awful lot like waking up from a nightmare. If you've been through something similar—escaped from a wild, traumatic experience like domestic abuse—then you know what I mean. Once you have complete separation from the abuse and are filled with relief and peace, it can feel like you were merely watching a movie of the events as a spectator from the outside. You try to forget as quickly as you can, brushing it aside and moving on as though it were all just a bad dream.

My mom made sure we were intentional about our healing process— she knew how important it was to break the cycle in order to keep us girls from following her footsteps into similar abusive situations down the line. We really leaned into it together, reading books and listening to tapes of motivational speakers and sermons. The summer before I started college was particularly rich with prayers, sermons, and reconnecting as a family. It was also during that summer that I took a step toward reclaiming my identity by legally changing my last name back to my father's. Soon after, declaring my intention to become an architect, I headed off to college—the ultimate opportunity to "find myself."

I wonder when you first felt the pull to reinvent yourself, to make your grand foray out into the world on your own. Maybe, like me, it happened when you left home for college; maybe you jumped headfirst into a cross-country move for the sake of your career, were forced to start fresh after the end of a relationship, or stumbled into some other turning point that disrupted everything you thought you knew. Maybe it's happened to you more than once—we often wind up reinventing ourselves several times throughout a lifetime!

What was one moment that helped you realize you wanted, or needed, a change? What internal shift told you it was time to become someone new, or to finally try to seek out who you really were all along?

I didn't know it then, as I yearned for the expansion of my world and identity through an escape to college, but the longing I felt—to find myself, to start over—wasn't just about running from the past. I believe it was the beginning of something deeper. Like a caterpillar beginning to feel the vague, internal stirrings of their eventual transformation, I dreamt of a kind of holy undoing. It was one of the earliest hints I was given of a God who doesn't just heal but lovingly reworks every torn and hidden part of us, like a master artist beginning the slow, sacred work of reassembly.

Having grown up all my life in the same small town in New Mexico, it's no wonder I dreamed of building my own adventure somewhere far, far away. I felt especially drawn toward New England and its elite Ivy League schools. After an overwhelming and exhilarating visit to

Boston and other areas of Massachusetts, I landed on Smith—a women's college where one of my mother's childhood friends happened to be a professor. Inspired by my grandmother and mom, who had spent years involved in a women's education organization called P.E.O., I saw the chance to be surrounded by strong women for my college years as a huge positive.

The career possibilities felt endless, and I loved that Smith, with its lack of core requirements, gave me leave to explore them all. That freedom fueled my curiosity, and I filled my schedule with classes spanning the gamut. I hadn't noticed, when choosing schools, that Smith didn't have an architecture program—whoops!—so I was registered as a music major at first. I had no interest in performing or teaching, but I kept the music classes up anyway, for the fun of it and for balance. Also drawn to languages and history, I switched from the French I had studied in high school to an equally impractical study of Italian, and I dove into a class on *The Canterbury Tales* in its original middle english dialect. At one point, I considered medieval studies. I suspect that my mother was quietly panicking about my future by this point, but she never discouraged me.

Most Smith students studied abroad junior year, but the idea of oral exams in Italian felt overwhelming, especially with ear infections still affecting my hearing. On top of that, Mom was putting three daughters through college by then, her personal expenses mounting, all while reinvesting in her business at the same time. So, I opted for a year of in-state tuition at the University of New Mexico, where my younger sister was just starting. It let us be in school together once again.

By then, I'd landed on psychology, especially the cognitive and developmental side. I loved studying how people think, how teams function, but my real drive was personal: I wanted to cure Alzheimer's (for my granddad, who by that point was lost deep in that horrible illness, my unflappable, stalwart grandmother by his side) and epilepsy (for my older sister). I briefly considered medical school, but the smell of formaldehyde had always made me physically ill. And with the political and societal landscape around health care shifting at the time, it didn't feel like a stable path.

So next, I turned to politics, hoping to make a difference that way. I applied for a Senate internship with Senator Pete Domenici and spent the summer doing real work—writing policy briefs and press releases, including one on WIC that was picked up by the media. It was eye-opening to see the realities of the legislative process. I took the LSAT and set my sights on law school.

College, for me, was a season of deep learning and constant redirection—from architecture to psychology to politics—always chasing the question: How can I make a difference? Where and how have you sought your own answer to that question, I wonder? Looking back at your own early adulthood, would you say you've ended up where you expected to go? Is that dream of making a difference still burning strong in your heart, fulfilled or not?

I want to encourage you: Don't limit yourself when you have those audacious dreams. God placed God-sized dreams in you because He wants you to shine. If you think you want to change the world, imagine how much He does too! I hope you'll trust Him to get you on the right path into joining in His good work.

Toward the end of my senior year, an opportunity arose: a student work exchange program in Ireland. I convinced my younger sister to join me—I would take a break before law school, and she would pause between the University of New Mexico and the Savannah College of Art and Design. We worked at my mom's business all that summer, saving every penny for the trip.

We were in for a rude awakening upon arrival. The support from the program proved to be minimal, and though we were provided with work visas, finding housing and employment turned out to be unexpectedly entirely our responsibility. We were essentially welcomed to the new country, handed newspapers with apartment and job listings circled, and told to find our own way! We got a reality check when it came to exchange rates, too—after exchanging all our savings, we received barely half the amount back in Irish pounds! It was sobering.

How often do we step into what feels like God's leading, only to find the path far more challenging than we expected? And yet, those are often the places where His deepest work begins.

For several weeks, we stayed in hostels, crammed into rooms full of bunk beds, sleeping on top of our bags with one eye open. One night, a wild-eyed woman with crazy hair and nothing but a T-shirt on came to my bed and started shaking my legs with all her might. I tried to stay perfectly still, pretending to sleep, silently praying she would move on. Eventually, we found a different hostel with private rooms and finally got some real rest.

After a bit of scrambling, we each found jobs at a small coffee shop, and with our combined wages, managed to rent a tiny flat. The "bedroom" was basically a converted closet with two built-in beds hugging opposite walls—just long enough for us, at 5'1" and 5'2", to fit if we lay perfectly straight, feet flexed, heads nearly touching the wall. It wasn't much, but it was ours.

The neighborhood itself was another surprise. Later, as we developed friendships at church, we learned that locals rolled up their windows and locked their doors when driving through that particular area. But even in the middle of tension—amidst bombings tied to the Northern Ireland conflict and a climate of Hatfields-and-McCoys revenge cycles—we saw God's protection covering us. Occasionally, during our hostel days, when we lugged our suitcases around with us wherever we went, people mistook us for locals and grew nervous when they saw us leaving our stuffed-full bags unattended, hackles raised under the constant fear of bomb threats. But then they'd hear our American accents and relax. There was a strange blend of innocence and danger all around us: stores closed on Sundays and strangers trusted us to watch their babies in McDonald's, even as the undercurrent of conflict simmered in the background.

As we navigated this new country, we were also navigating new spiritual ground. Coming from a conservative Southern Baptist background, we were feeling drawn toward something more charismatic. Someone told us about a church that was part of the Vineyard Movement, an offshoot of the "Toronto Blessing," or (as I heard it called later) the "laughing revival." That first name caught my attention immediately, given that my mom's business back home was called The Vineyard. It felt like one of those God-winks, a small reminder that He's always weaving the pieces of the story together.

The church itself was unlike anything I had experienced. Services took place in a Catholic church building, and they weren't confined to one hour on Sunday; they would last all day, full of worship, music, teaching, and prayer tinged with the vibrancy of a charismatic revival. What struck me most was how spiritually dry everything around us—really the culture of the U.K. in general—had felt up until then. Like parched, cracked ground that needed a soaking rain, the Spirit was being poured out again and again through that movement, softening dry hearts and stoic pride through both laughter and tears, turning a parched desert into a lush garden.

We saw miracles firsthand. A woman who had been deaf regained her hearing. Another woman, who dealt with multiple mental disabilities, was suddenly devouring books and talking about aerodynamics and aerospace with remarkable clarity. God was deeply restoring bodies, minds, hearts, and souls.

That season was incredibly transformational for me, and for my sister as well. When we returned to the States, she was able to break free from destructive relationships and find deep healing in a way that changed the trajectory of her life. For both of us, it was a time of unusual closeness, shared faith, and a front-row seat to the mystery of how God can pour out His Spirit and make dry places flourish.

Looking back, I see that period of my life as a reminder that God uses every single piece of your story as He shapes and reshapes, directs and calls you. He doesn't waste anything! Away from home during college—and especially when I was off in a whole new country and experiencing God in a whole new way—I was also gaining a deeper understanding of and appreciation for my upbringing, heritage, and identity, all those parts of myself I had taken for granted before. He was weaving together every thread of my story, even then, quietly guiding me through the twists and turns and drawing me together into something whole.

As you reflect on your own journey, are you able to think of moments when space from your roots solidified the way those roots continue to live and breathe in who you are today?

Where can you see God's fingerprints? Really feel Him moving, acting, and touching your heart?

What moments felt random at the time but were actually part of a greater tapestry? Where has He been shaping you, even when you didn't recognize it?

I wonder.

PART 2
Molting

CHAPTER 4

When Everything Falls Apart

DID YOU KNOW a caterpillar's final disintegration and recreation in the cocoon isn't the only dramatic physical change that it goes through? As it prepares for that total and final transformation, it first enters a long season of molting. It grows (much like its most famous literary member, the Very Hungry Caterpillar) until it is absolutely bursting from its restrictive skin. So, it sheds it—and then grows some more—and sheds again—over and over and over—throwing off each outer shell that no longer fits, expanding and maturing, coming closer and closer to its final metamorphosis.

I suspect you'll understand what I mean when I say that many of us humans experience something similar in our own journeys. I certainly did. My first true "molting," when I felt my identity being painfully shed for something new, came when my mom's business fell apart. The Vineyard had been a constant presence since childhood, and it may as well have gone up in a puff of smoke.

I said before that The Vineyard was an enterprise sparked by desperation, but it was my mother's inspiration that fanned the flame and kept it alive. From the very beginning, it was a project grounded in purpose, community, and the goal of creating something beautiful and meaningful. This approach to business would deeply inspire me in my own career later in life. The Vineyard's earliest products—works of matted, framed calligraphy art often featuring Bible verses—reflected the faith that underpinned my mother's vision. When she and her business partner added in fabric-covered frames as well, the leftover material from the centers was cleverly repurposed into small, embroidered wall plaques. Every detail mattered, and just like in God's work in our own stories and lives, nothing was wasted.

I spent much of my childhood surrounded by bolts of fabric and spools of ribbon. My sisters and I helped wherever we could: vacuuming the front office (which taught me the painful patience of detangling threads from the vacuum roller every few minutes), cutting foam with an electric turkey knife to stuff bows, and learning to perfectly tape shipping boxes in an "H" pattern to pass drop tests. As we grew, my mom taught us that, as the children of the owners, we had to work the hardest, set the example, and do every job with excellence—no matter how small. It all shaped my work ethic and my understanding of leadership far more than I realized at the time.

Her business partner, who handled sales and marketing, had gone through a divorce, then remarried. When her new husband joined the business, it introduced complications that would later create fractures. But for many years, it worked. My mom, on the operational and design side, focused on the factory, finances, process and product design. They eventually moved the headquarters to Dallas and opened a second factory there during my college years, while my mom remained in New Mexico to run the original location.

One of the earliest stories I remember about The Vineyard is when my mother and her business partner took their products to the Dallas Gift Market for the first time. Audaciously optimistic, they packed thousands of printed order forms—so many they had to lug them in suitcases heavy as bags of concrete. When they arrived, the men helping with their bags nearly pulled their arms out of the sockets. And only upon arriving did they discover the market provided its own order forms. What's more, they wound up receiving barely any orders, anyway. But all those leftover order forms wound up providing us with excellent scratch paper for years, and the story was always told with a chuckle.

Speaking of which: I've always tended to be quite serious and intense, but it was my mother who taught me to try to find the humor and light even in the worst moments. She also taught me to laugh at myself and not take myself so seriously! I wonder if you relate, and if glimmers of joy have ever carried you through your own dark times. Humor has certainly been a bright thread through my own hardest trials, making the slog bearable and helping me keep my eyes fixed on hope with the reminder of how temporary our feelings and troubles really are. When given the choice between laughter and tears? Choose laughter.

Rather than give up after that trying experience at the Dallas Gift Market, my mom came home and designed a full line of fabric-covered items over the course of a couple short, inspired months. Shortly afterward, things really began to grow. The business moved from the garage to an old Kentucky Fried Chicken building we lovingly called "the shop." I remember helping build the shipping shelves and watching Mom design a structured, color-coded order system with her trademark rigor and innovation.

Building a business also brought along risks and setbacks, like the time they tried to haul home a load of discounted glass in a pickup truck. It cut through the ropes securing it, shattering across four lanes of traffic. The entire road had to be shut down, and not a single piece was salvageable because what wasn't broken had skidded, scratching the surface of the glass with road rash. I imagine that was a deeply frustrating moment, but it, too, became one of those family stories we told with laughter for years to come.

One of the most meaningful turns in the business came when they needed to hire workers and were connected to an organization helping a group of Laotian refugees who had recently lost their jobs when a Levi's factory closed. These were families who had fled communism—some literally crossing rivers under fire, having friends and family members killed, and leaving loved ones behind. As they came into the business, they often prayed over the work and for the business itself. They stretched our minds and hearts as they introduced us all to a cross-cultural experience that was rare indeed in our small, Bible Belt town.

I still remember the joy in my mother's face as she said one day, "When I was a girl, I felt called to be a missionary in Africa, but I didn't go. So, God brought the mission field to me!" The relationship we built with that refugee community came to mean so much to her. The business became not just a job, but a ministry—something we all viewed as being laden with spiritual depth and purpose. And that wasn't new in our family. The foundation had been laid long before: my granddad a church deacon and dentist who served on medical mission trips, my grandmother a Sunday school teacher, and my mom filling in at churches across the area when they needed an organist or pianist.

So many lessons were embedded in those years: resilience, purpose, leadership. Even crises like the wave of carpal tunnel claims that almost shut down the business brought opportunities. With help, they moved employees under a larger Texas company and leased them back, averting disaster and paving the way for expansion. It was always about finding a way forward, even when the road was rough.

Throughout my breaks from school during college, I continued to help out with the business, just as I had since I was a child. After returning from Ireland, I caught wind of a law school scholarship available to New Mexico students attending SMU Law School in Dallas. Since my mom's business had a location there as well, I decided to make the move to Texas and see how I liked it. Over that summer, my mom had attended her thirty-year high school reunion and ran into her junior high sweetheart. They were both single and began to fall in love all over again. So, this man (who would later become my dad) wound up helping me make the move from New Mexico to a new apartment in the Dallas-Fort Worth area.

What began as a temporary job working for The Vineyard in Dallas gradually shifted into something full time. Even though I was fully capable of pursuing law school, I realized that path didn't fit the way I was wired. It wasn't work I would love. So instead, I stayed at the Dallas location of my mother's business and leaned into the work right in front of me. Sometimes we're called to get up and go, serving God in strange new worlds. But so often, we're called to lean into and give back to the communities we already find ourselves in. Don't you think?

Oh, what a growing experience it was! I had started learning entry-level cost accounting from my mother and expanded that learning under the CFO, eventually building out product bill-of-materials systems that could later be integrated into a full manufacturing ERP system. I picked up unexpected skills as I went and wound up helping with the system migration, submitting invoices to our largest client through an early Electronic Data Interchange system—primitive compared to the smooth online invoicing we have now. When files failed, there was no simple way to resubmit, so I also worked alongside our tech staff to learn the programming language and write code to recover those flawed invoices, ensuring we got paid.

Most people at the company didn't realize I was the daughter of one of the owners. I simply came in quietly and worked hard, often staying late to finish projects that would help the business. My mom had always modeled that steady humility and diligence, and I strove to follow in her footsteps.

During that season, my dad proposed to my mom, and they decided to hold the wedding in Dallas. I was the only family member living there at the time, so my focus shifted for a while as I helped with flowers, planning, and all the details that go into blending two families. And

God, in His grace, wove even more people into our story, as my mom gained two new stepdaughters who fit into the family like missing puzzle pieces. The ceremony was small but full of love and laughter. Sometimes it's the things that don't go exactly according to plan that end up becoming the sweetest memories.

Not long after, the atmosphere at work began to shift. I had been praying hard, interceding intensely for my mom and her business partners as the relationships between the three of them began to fray and strain. There were difficult conversations happening behind closed doors and plenty of questionable decisions being made. I often found myself feeling caught in the middle, which I absolutely hated. My mom and I could both see that an unraveling was underway. There was a betrayal unfolding in a slow and complicated way, wounding deeply precisely because of how deep the friendships had once been. What had felt like a covenant relationship when The Vineyard began had now become something very different.

I wonder if you've ever experienced that kind of fracturing in a relationship. If so, I am so sorry.

And then came a moment that I will never forget. In the middle of my praying and pleading for God to fix what was broken, He spoke to me in a voice that was firm and unmistakable: "Stop interceding. They've made their choices, and it's time to move on. You need to leave."

There was no room for hesitation. I faxed in my resignation immediately and began sending out my résumé, not knowing where I would land, only knowing that it was time to move forward. When God says it's time to go, you don't stay and try to negotiate, do you?

My mom remained for a time, working to create the cleanest exit possible. Eventually, she decided to let her partners buy her out. They wanted the Clovis factory closed and to consolidate operations in Dallas. My parents planned to move to Austin, looking forward to an early retirement and what was supposed to be a new beginning.

But instead, it became a different kind of wilderness. After the exit, my mother didn't end up getting a dime. Her business partners bankrupted her instead. Her lawyers failed spectacularly throughout the process, and she was left personally liable for enormous business debts. My parents had lost her salary, the business, and all their retirement plans in one fell swoop.

Growing up in a small town like Clovis made the situation even harder. There was no such thing as faceless creditors; the people my mother was now in deep, personal debt to were people she knew. She was also under a non-compete clause, unable to start fresh in the industry she had built her life around.

By that point, my parents had already headed off to Austin, where things weren't much better. My dad's real estate license from New Mexico wasn't valid in Texas yet. And Austin, filled with tech startups, offered few open doors for either of them.

It was such a heartbreaking loss, and the betrayal was painful in a way that reached to our bones. Even though, in one sense, I was watching the tragedy and collapse happen to my mother, it was happening to me too. This thing our family had been grounded on for so long was gone. So much trust had been broken, so much pain caused. The injuries to my heart left it crippled, thinking all partnerships were bad, and that I would never want to be in one with the possibility of such treachery. Around this time, I let pieces of myself die.

Have you ever walked through a season where so much collapses at once, you struggle to even recognize who you are anymore? When entire portions of your identity feel completely stripped away?

Even during that horrible time for my parents, God provided in outrageous ways. At one point, my mom found an entire case of beef tenderloin marked down at the grocery store—high-quality meat somehow made cheaper than any other meat in the store. She filled an upright freezer in their garage. There was so much filet mignon that not only were my parents eating it regularly, but so were the dogs, stray cats, and even the neighborhood possums! At night, my dad would grill, and the animals would line up along the patio wall, waiting for their portion.

Another time, Mom filled her grocery cart with chickens that had discount stickers on them. At the register, after all the coupons were applied, instead of having to pay at all, she was given money back!

"You prepare a table before me in the presence of my enemies…"[2] God provided lavishly even in the middle of heartbreak, in ways that almost seemed absurd, as if to remind us: "I am still here. I see you."

In the middle of all this, my granddad's health declined. His Alzheimer's had been worsening since I was in high school, but now it was clear we were near the end. My grandmother bore it all with her quiet, stiff-upper-lip strength, but none of us fully understood how much she was carrying behind the scenes, or how dangerous some of those moments had become as Granddad's strength and confusion collided.

He passed away while I was still trying to find my footing after leaving the business. Shortly after, my mom's childhood best friend, Merle, died suddenly in a tragic accident following years of migraine struggles. Our families had grown up together; our moms were best friends, our grandmothers too. We daughters had shared so many sweet, carefree childhood memories. It was another sharp loss, stacked on top of everything else.

There are seasons when the losses come one after another, where grief feels layered and unrelenting, when survival mode is all you have left. When everything that defined your "before" life seems to belong to someone else entirely. I think of Joseph imprisoned for so many years in Pharaoh's court, and of the Israelites wandering under the hot sun.

But these are often the places where God begins the slow, painful rearrangement of our identity. I truly believe that He allows certain things to die so He can resurrect what was never meant to be built on shaky ground.

Have you lived through that kind of stripping? When everything stable crumbles and you are left to trust that somehow God is still working

---

2. Psalm 23:5

beneath the rubble? Can you look back now and see the faint outlines of His provision, His mercy, even in the most impossible circumstances?

This was certainly not the end of the story. But it was a pivotal moment, a tearing down before the building up could truly begin. The identity I once carried had to be dismantled, piece by piece, to make room for what God was preparing to rebuild. I was headed squarely into a season of heavy molting.

CHAPTER 5

A New Season

UPON LEAVING MY work at The Vineyard, with its bent toward accounting and computer programming, I found myself at a fork in the road. I've often looked back at that time and wondered what on earth my life might have looked like if I'd chosen a different career path—if I had decided to follow my feet straight into accounting, for example. I wonder if you, too, can think of those times when you stood at a crossroads, unable to see past the bends in any of the winding, diverging paths ahead of you. I know, even in that uncertainty, even if you look back from time to time with curiosity or regret, God was there with you all along, watching over you and weaving all things together for good.

I have excelled at math my whole life, finding math contests and puzzles good fun even as a child; after all, it's in my DNA! My grandmother was a junior high math teacher, and my mom was a math whiz herself. Our highly developed spatial abilities showed up clearly, even in the way we packed our vacation coolers with the precision of mathematicians—layering frozen meat wrapped in foil and newspaper—as well as how we packed suitcases and people into every crevice of the car for trips to the cabin in the New Mexico mountains.

Yet my interests have also always extended beyond logic and numbers. I am one of those odd birds who thrives equally in both left-brain logic and right-brain creativity. To this day, I still rarely tell others about what I consider the third part of my brain—that intuitive, emotive space where ideas seem to arrive from some distant galaxy and slowly take shape in isolation from either right- or left-brained thinking, unattached to words or pictures at all. Often, I can't fully explain what I'm seeing in my head until I simply build or design it, watching puzzled stares turn to understanding as vision becomes reality.

Growing up in a family of visionaries trained me well for that kind of forward-thinking creativity. My mom, always ahead of fashion trends, had us wearing new styles with confidence long before they were popular. My sisters and I experimented with our own designs, too—my older sister wore nothing but business suits one year, and my younger sister created handmade hats out of hatboxes. Once, in high school, I decided to create a pencil skirt that fit me like a glove, so I traced myself onto the fabric to create the pattern. (Unfortunately, it turned out one inch too small in every direction, since I forgot to account for seam allowances). My granddad, who once dreamed of becoming a fashion designer, passed that love of fabrics and fine details on to us.

My point here is that my interests, paths, and goals have always ranged widely all over the map, making this particular "fork in the road" moment a difficult one for me. In general, I knew that my goals tended to orbit a few constants: helping people, simplifying complexity, adding beauty, and making the world a better place, with bonus points for anything including adventure, creativity, and laughter. And my overarching life goal has always been to develop as many diverse talents as possible, reflecting God's creativity and glory back into the world.

How have your interests, talents, and goals directed, anchored, or expanded your own experience of life? When you reflect on the giftings and passions that have burned in your heart throughout the many phases of your life, are you able to see the threads continuing to glimmer here and there today? Can you see how they led you to where you are now? I wonder.

In my case, as I stood at this career crossroads, it was eventually technology that drew me in. Software programming allowed space for both structure and artistry. It allowed for creative problem-solving, architectural design, and innovation. When a specialized tax accounting firm needed a software developer, it felt like the perfect fit for the next phase of my life.

A caterpillar will shed and molt, depending on the species, four to five times during its brief existence in that unwinged form. The periods between moltings are called instars, and each one reveals a slightly different version of the caterpillar and a new stage of growth. The final breaking down and reassembly, of course, won't occur until the cocoon, but those new layers certainly mean something—certainly feel significant—as they happen.

This period was one of my instar stages, a new layer of growth, the beginnings of rearranging and reweaving. I transitioned from the stage lights and music performances of my youth to a quiet, behind-the-scenes corporate life. Those memories of piano recitals, gymnastics meets, choir tours, and band performances got tucked neatly into a drawer of forgetfulness, and I leaned into my new, career-centered identity with gusto.

I wonder if you can recognize the instar stages in your own life. If you aren't sure, think back: When could you feel yourself shedding old layers and stepping into new ones?

Molting pains aside, I thrived in my new role. After just one year at the firm, I won employee of the year, earning a bonus trip of my choice. I invited my grandmother to join me for a week in Italy and Monaco. We traveled by train, explored beautiful cities, journaled, and captured memories in photos that I later turned into a keepsake album. It was a sweet gift for both of us during a season that felt something like stability after so much upheaval.

During those years, life quietly moved forward. My older sister moved to Dallas, and we became roommates. A friend from work and I began working out together, and I even dabbled in rock climbing after a brief introduction from a guy I dated. My younger sister married and moved to California, and when I visited her, the allure of California living tugged at me (though the cost of living held me back). For a time, it felt like all of us were searching for our footing, each in our own way, working out how to "do our own things" after growing up so deeply intertwined with the family business.

In truth, we were all molting. Our old identities were falling away, and we were changing and maturing, as was only natural. My older sister tried her hand at various sales positions. My younger sister built a new life across the country. And I quietly worked through my own layers of guardedness. I had always been slow to warm up to people, cautious with my heart, needing time to trust. I wonder if you relate—if you have your guard up in some area, an area where God may just be inviting you into deeper trust and openness to His guidance?

This healing was steady, quiet work happening beneath the surface, rearranging old wounds and defenses, and it all came to a head when I met the man who would be my husband.

It was St. Patrick's Day, 2001. A friend and I were visiting my parents in Austin and decided, on a whim, to go down to Sixth Street. We rarely went out like that, but something about the night felt different. As we ate at a restaurant, we ran into two guys who were also visiting the city. They invited us to go dancing with them. And somehow, all of us ended up marrying each other.

I didn't marry my husband right away. He was ready before I was. Marriage brought its own set of wounds for me to work through, and it took time for my heart to fully open. But by 2006, both my older sister and I were married within months of each other, and yet another new season began.

CHAPTER 6

Dreams Deferred

HOPE IS A wonderful thing; I strive to walk through life with hope, because how would I ever have gotten through without the expectation that God was guiding me toward something bright and beautiful, His hand wrapped firmly and warmly around mine? What a glorious thought.

There are times, though, when we bypass hope entirely and instead simply expect that the path ahead will unfold the way we want it to—or at least the way it did for those around us. Does that sound familiar at all? Think of a newly married couple, setting their sights on what we tend to consider the "next step" after the wedding: the start of a family. They begin trying for a baby, set up the nursery, and buy the teeny-tiny clothes with love already blossoming in their hearts.

For me, that specific flavor of hope seemed reasonable. My sisters had both become pregnant easily, even when faced with minor hurdles. I assumed that once my own husband moved into the house, pregnancy would soon follow.

But sometimes the caterpillar does not molt in the way we expect it to.

Even before I got married, I had begun to prepare for the possibility of children. A close friend of mine, that same friend who had met her husband the night I met mine, had been diagnosed with fibroid tumors and visited a fertility specialist to (successfully!) preserve her options for pregnancy. Not long after that, I too discovered fibroid tumors and turned to the same specialist, even though I was not yet married. As we discussed my situation and prepared for the surgical removal of the tumors, my doctor recommended testing for thrombophilia due to my family's history of pulmonary embolisms. The tests came back negative for me, but later, when my younger sister became pregnant with her second child, I encouraged her to get tested as well. She did and tested positive. With careful monitoring and medication, she safely carried her pregnancy through.

By the time I was married, both of my sisters had already entered motherhood—one getting pregnant almost immediately after her wedding, the other carefully monitored but successful. Meanwhile, I set up my own nursery and began to wait for my turn, expectant and excited.

But the months of waiting stretched into years. We pursued fertility treatments, and I underwent multiple surgeries: two to remove the fibroids and one to correct a uterine septum, a condition where the uterus had not fully formed as it should have. Each procedure felt like another molt, another painful shedding of expectations. Yet even with all these treatments, the door to natural pregnancy remained closed.

There was only one moment during those years when I let the full weight of grief break through, a time when I allowed myself a brief taste of painful, risky hope. I was so sure that this time, finally, I might actually be pregnant. All the signs were pointing to yes! When that breathlessly awaited test came back negative, I cried my heart out.

But for the most part, I held it all tightly inside. I stayed stoic, practical, shielding my heart behind carefully constructed walls. If I didn't allow myself to feel the highs, I reasoned, then perhaps I wouldn't feel the lows so deeply either.

Are there places where you, too, have built protective walls around your heart?

I was trying to protect myself from the pain. But in doing so, I hardened parts of my heart I didn't even realize I was closing off. It was only later—much later—that God gently returned to those places and began the slow work of healing them, peeling back the layers, helping me feel again, teaching me the value of the whole, wide range of the human experience, pains and joys alike.

Eventually, my husband and I considered using a gestational carrier, but the cost, the risks, and the ethical complexities of the process weighed heavily on us. After years of treatments and expenses, we just couldn't justify the financial and emotional toll.

We also explored adoption, but because of our age, the years spent pursuing other solutions, and the increasing restrictions and corruption in some international adoption systems, that door closed as well. Countries that had once welcomed adoptive families were tightening their borders or revealed troubling practices. We even looked into becoming foster parents, and I still remember opening the agency's website and being overwhelmed by page after page of forms—a three-ring binder's worth of documentation. The system was so broken, placing impossible demands on good foster parents while allowing repeated chances for abusive or neglectful biological parents. Friends of ours shared stories that left us heartbroken and discouraged. Eventually, we realized that the emotional rollercoaster of fostering, where children might be returned again and again to unstable situations, would have been too devastating for us.

And so, after many years of trying every path we could find, we surrendered. There would be no children. The nursery sat empty, and we finally accepted that the chapter we had hoped for would never be written in the way we imagined.

If you are reading this as someone who has struggled with infertility and childlessness (or if you care about someone who has dealt with these struggles) my heart goes out to you. Know that we are in good company, that the Bible is full of women who wept to God for a child, and that whether we experience miracles or not, God is weeping with us. I pray you are able to trust in His plan for you, and that He steadily guides you to other ways to pour out your tender, motherly love on those around you.

Have you ever had door after door slammed shut? When the object of your hope seems out of reach, so you try every avenue you can think of, unsure whether to keep fighting or give in? I pray that, for you, the journey ended in fulfillment—or that, when you eventually accepted that the dream would not come to be, you felt God's peace and were able (after the grief subsided) to rest in your knowledge of His goodness and His perfect plan.

As my husband and I let go of our dream of raising a family together, we embraced a new dream. We poured our love into our nieces and nephews, into each other, and into the life God had given us.

Take a moment to look back on your own deferred and denied dreams, whether the pain is fresh and sharp or old and dulling. How did that thwarted hope shape and form your journey? What might it look like to allow God to gently begin healing and transforming those places where the story didn't go quite the way you expected?

CHAPTER 7

The Entrepreneurial Years

J'D LIKE TO take a moment to speak to the business leaders and entrepreneurs reading this book.

We've talked a lot about identity so far—how we form it and how we shed it, how God lovingly preserves and repairs the broken pieces. If you've found yourself drawn into business ownership and leadership, chances are you are chock-full of God-given passion and drive for what you do. That's wonderful! But there's a shadow side. Entrepreneurship can easily take over and come to define you completely, as you let your identity become so entwined with what you do that you forget how to rest in God, to lean on Him as your primary source of identity. Sound familiar at all?

Humans in general struggle to separate their sense of worth and value from their performance, but oh man. There's not much that makes it quite as difficult as being an entrepreneur.

I'd already seen that lesson play out in my mother's life, as she dealt with the disorientation of her exit from The Vineyard, and soon enough, I found myself facing my own challenges around identity and work-life balance.

By 2010 I was still working full-time in IT, spending long days in the office writing software and managing projects, but I'd given over my evenings and weekends to entrepreneurship. If you're wondering how I found time to simply breathe and be in the midst of all that… well. Good question. I didn't, really.

My husband, who has a background in physical therapy, had also been coaching All Star cheer on the side. He'd competed in college cheer himself—on one of our earliest dates, I actually flew to Orlando to watch his team place second at nationals—and he wanted to do more with that passion. Our hearts were ready and open for "something new" after finally surrendering our dream of having children, so we decided to launch a cheerleading program of our own. We had plenty of vision and enthusiasm, which certainly counted for something, but we didn't have a building or even a set team.

I still remember the little Honda Accord I used to haul everything around in: banker boxes stuffed with uniforms, makeup kits, T-shirts, paperwork. Every weekend, I'd pack the car up and head to the gym while he coached. I was the coat rack, the photographer, the office manager. I eventually bought a backpack with wheels just so I could get everything to and from competitions without killing my shoulders. It was laps and laps around stadium floors, carting gear for one team, then circling back for the next.

We had such a heart for the beginners, those kids who were just discovering the sport. We poured everything we had into building them up, giving them confidence, discipline, and resilience. Some of them stuck around. A lot of them eventually went on to bigger, more competitive gyms. We kind of wound up being the "get them started off on the right foot" gym. We loved that role, but the model made things tough when it came to actually running a sustainable business.

At the same time, around 2012, I started helping my mom and sister with a project of their own. My sister was living in Ohio, and she and my mom had come up with the idea of upscale scarves that doubled as ponchos. She loved fashion and had a knack for sales; my mom had business experience and design ideas; and I offered to help with the tech and back-office stuff.

On weekends when I wasn't at the gym, I was at my mom's house in the Dallas area, setting up mannequins, photographing scarves, uploading products to Shopify, handling the website, email marketing, and online store management. It was new, creative work that I genuinely enjoyed... but it never, ever stopped. Between the cheer gym and the scarf business, there were simply no free hours left in my life.

Plus, we weren't even making any money. Most of the weekends I dedicated to the scarf business cost more than they actually earned. I'd cram the car full of boxes and mannequins, set up booths at local markets, and sometimes we'd only sell one $30 scarf. A measly profit, especially split three ways!

By 2016 or 2017, both businesses had run their course and closed down. We'd learned some incredible lessons along the way, about perseverance and creativity, but at the time it was hard to see the situation as anything but pure failure. I had poured years of time, energy, money, and heart into both enterprises, and I couldn't help wondering what their slow deaths said about me. Even more than that, it was off-putting to realize how much of my identity had gotten wrapped up in those projects. It was yet another painful molting, another shedding of identity along my path toward the cocoon.

I wonder if you've ever experienced something similar, tying yourself tightly to your work and then being forced to find yourself again once your circumstances changed. Have you ever gotten so wrapped up in what you do, whether you're succeeding or not, that you forgot your deepest identity could be found in God?

Again, entrepreneurship has a way of getting under your skin. For all the innate goodness of having a heart and drive for building a business, if you're not careful, your identity will start to get blurred and smudged together with your productivity, slowly overlapping till you don't feel like you're anybody in particular outside of your business. It happens to all of us at some point—we start to believe that what we do is who we are. It makes it impossibly easy, and even inevitable, to lose our bearings.

I've had to learn how to untangle my worth from my work more than once since then. Looking back, I can now see how much I actually gained from those years. I learned how to build email campaigns and online stores. I learned social media marketing and small-business accounting. I learned how to lead with both heart and strategy. God was building a toolkit I would one day need.

And maybe even more than that, He was shaping my character—reminding me to view the world through a lens of gratitude, acknowledging what others were contributing in the moments when I began to feel bitter about the workload I had to manage behind the scenes. This season taught me to see the body of Christ in action and reminded me that we need all the parts working together in order to get anything done.

That's one of the things I still really love about entrepreneurship: It gives you the chance to love people from top to bottom. If you're the boss and you don't want to scrub the toilets? Then you'd better be ready to thank the janitor. You'd better be ready to love everyone along the way.

I guess what I'd say to you business leaders out there is just this: Be wary. Pay attention to signs that you're drifting into an unhealthy balance and false sense of identity. When you're chasing vision after vision, trying to hold everything together, grasping at "success," it's too easy to find yourself disconnecting from the people you love, and even from God.

Over the last few years, that's one of the biggest things God has been working on in me. He's been restoring my trust in partnership, rebalancing my identity, and showing me that survival mode isn't the goal. Christ-rooted abundance is the abundance that comes as God weaves you together along the way.

And that brings us to the cocoon.

PART 3

Cocoon

CHAPTER 8

The Eye of the Storm

I HAVE NO IDEA what it feels like when a caterpillar enters a cocoon. Does it hurt when it dissolves into goop, is rearranged in the darkness, and breaks back out into the light again as an entirely new, yet glimmeringly familiar, creature? I don't think modern science has quite answered that question yet.

I do know that my own metamorphosis was no easy process, though. It was a time of uncertainty and disorientation and shadows, yet also filled with the growing certainty that the mosaic of me was still there. All the shards of my past and my dreams and the truest pieces of who I was coming together under God's good and mysterious timing.

I wonder if you've experienced your own cocooning yet, or are in the midst of it, or can see hints of it around the bend. Wherever you are in this process of being broken down and rewoven, take heart. God is with you, and He is guiding you through.

My time in the cocoon truly began around 2017, as my mom, my sisters, and I felt called to start praying together for restoration. We leaned into a strong, shared sense that something was about to shift—that the pain from The Vineyard's disintegration twenty years earlier would finally be healed, that there would be a breakthrough, and that what had been taken would, somehow, be recovered. I can only continue to believe now that this impulse was God-given, perhaps as a protective measure, drawing us into sweet communion and closeness that would comfort us through everything that came next.

I believe He was also preparing us in other ways. I was feeling deeply discouraged in my work at the time and essentially begging God for a green light to quit. Instead, He guided me to turn my energy toward encouraging others. Skeptical at feeling His pull in this direction, while I was so hopelessly in the depths of discouragement myself, I did something unusual for me. I called a prayer line. The person on the other end shared this message (unprompted!): "I believe God wants you to send encouragement to others during this time."

Well! You don't need to tell me… thrice, I suppose. Thank God for His patience with my (more than occasional) stubbornness!

I started out by simply emailing my closest family members a daily Bible verse or positive quote and quickly found that when you give encouragement to others, it flows back to you, filling you with hope and joy. I see now how God ultimately used that life-giving practice to help us all stay afloat during the upcoming storms. I know that I couldn't have gotten through what came next without having been strengthened by that season of shared encouragement.

God sure does know what He's doing, doesn't He? When you reflect on your own darkest moments, your own cocoon, can you see the ways He quietly laid a firm foundation for you, fortified you, and shored up your provisions for the hardship around the bend?

Over the course of the next few years, my family didn't exactly experience the restoration we'd expected. Instead, all hell broke loose, and we found ourselves flung into a whirlpool of tragedies and almost-tragedies.

First, my uncle was diagnosed with lung cancer. He was at an age where he didn't yet qualify for Medicare, so being in general good health (especially given the huge cost of regular health insurance), he had gone without it entirely. This added an additional layer of stress on top of his diagnosis and led to delays that allowed the tumor to grow to the size of a softball by the time he was able to have surgery. MRIs showed a single cancerous mass in his lung, and at one point my mom had a vision of God's hands around that tumor, preventing it from spreading any further. That is what we began to pray for most regularly during that time, often and fervently.

My uncle had recently moved to the Dallas area to be closer to my grandmother, parents, and me, but he lived alone. So my mom—his sister—and I rallied around him, becoming his caregivers and encouragers. I printed out a binder of encouraging quotes and pictures to buoy us, one of which showed our beautiful blue and green Earth with God's hand cradling it, alongside words that would come to be my own personal, sustaining rallying cry—not only during that time but throughout the other hard parts of my life to come: "God's got this."

And indeed, He did. When my uncle was finally able to undergo surgery, my mom and I sat in the waiting room for ten hours, receiving infrequent, brief, often indecipherable updates like, "He's in the mesh stage!" (Huh? We only found out what they were talking about later: The tumor had wrapped itself around his ribs, so three of them had to be removed entirely, and a major thoracic nerve had to be severed. Your ribs not only provide structure and stability to your body, but they also surround your organs for protection. Without this, mesh was needed to keep his organs in place. The mesh didn't provide any structural stability, although we did tease him later that it felt like he had been put back together with chicken wire.)

Bill spent so much time in the ICU recovering after that. Quite frequently he was moved overnight to a new room, so we laughed that attendants must have nightly hospital bed races, rearranging patients just for fun. But he was due to be released just in time for Thanksgiving dinner, and truly, we had so much to be thankful for.

My other uncle, Ed, had flown into town to see Bill and spend the holiday with all of us. However, that day, it turned out that Bill had developed an infection. We were deeply disappointed that he wouldn't be released, but staying in the hospital to treat the infection saved his life. If he had been at home, it may not have been caught in time.

When Bill was finally released and we returned for the post-op and biopsy report, the doctor gravely told us that my uncle was riddled with late-stage cancer. Feeling stunned and a bit terrified, all I could do was whisper to my mom and uncle, "God's got this!" Then the doctor turned to the chart and read through each line item. "Lymph node one, no cancer. Lymph node two, no cancer. Rib one, no cancer in the bone, no cancer in the marrow. Rib two, no cancer in the bone, no cancer in the marrow. Rib three…"

When she reached the end of the page, having declared every part of my uncle's body free and clear, she paused. "I'm sorry, I was mistaken. You are cancer free." Praise God.

On top of my uncle's journey with cancer, my grandmother ended up with a compression fracture in her back. She went from being a ninety-year-old in good health and mental acuity to experiencing a rapid decline.

My mom's other brother, too, suffered a grave accident. He had been riding horses with his wife in the mountains when the horse's hoof slipped on a rock, throwing him off while leaving him still partially tangled in the stirrup. As much as the horse tried not to, it began stepping all over him in an effort not to fall. My aunt had to rush back to a place where she could get cell reception and notified all of us to start praying. Miraculously, he sustained no broken bones or internal injuries, but for months afterward, bruises in the shape of horseshoes would come to the surface, a reminder of his near-death experience.

My younger sister then tore the ACL in her knee, requiring a cadaver donor ligament to repair. Her son, my nephew, was being goofy with friends when he got pushed off a wall onto his head and shoulders, narrowly escaping a broken neck, and his sister, my niece, got pneumonia. With severe allergies to almost every antibiotic possible, she was admitted to a hospital which had specialized services to find something that would eliminate the infection in a way her body could tolerate.

My older sister also had what we thought was a major grand mal seizure, falling in a way that left her with black eyes. Later, a test revealed that most likely it had been a stroke, given the evidence seen in the CAT scan, rather than a seizure.

In a short time, almost the entire family on my mom's side was nearly wiped out. Thank God for all of His miracles.

But the trials didn't end with just those family members. My husband's grandmother had various falls and ultimately died. A month later, my own grandmother died from all the complications of her back injury. Around the same time as my niece's illness, my husband also got pneumonia, despite there being half the country's distance between Texas and Pennsylvania. My dad then had a reverse shoulder replacement, and my husband's father got melanoma, though he was fortunately able to get a new breakthrough personalized medical treatment. Just as he was recovering, he also got a MRSA infection, along with, at some point, having a stroke!

After my grandmother's death and burial in Clovis, our family decided to hold a family reunion in Red River to celebrate her life. As I was preparing for that trip, one of my cats died suddenly of a heart attack. While grief for people is deeper, losing a pet on top of everything else was a daily reminder of sorrow during that time.

On the anniversary of my grandmother's birthday, after her death, my mom called in the middle of the night because her blood pressure had spiked to almost double the normal range. My sisters and I began to pray, and once my mom was finally seen at the emergency room, we were relieved to hear that, by the grace of God, she did not have a stroke.

It was such a torrent that it felt almost ridiculous. I found myself unable to even tell people about the sheer volume of what we were facing, because I was sure they would think I was either crazy or lying! That Job-like time remains an intense blur in my memory. I wonder if you've ever experienced a "Job moment" like this yourself, and whether you felt as overwhelmed as I did. I wonder if you were able to seek and find God's steady presence in the midst of all the noise and worry and pain. I hope so.

Outside this tornado of family difficulties lay yet another whirlwind. It began when my company was carved out of our parent company and restructured just two weeks before the whole world shut down due to the COVID-19 pandemic. I had been working in software development and program management up to that point, but when our IT director quit in October 2020, several months into the pandemic, I accepted a high-pressure leadership position. I quickly went from being a specialist to learning the ropes of hardware and network servers.

When that happened, I remember driving up to our office building with the song "Jericho" by Andrew Ripp playing on the radio, and it became my rallying cry of the moment.

The office had become a ghost town during the shutdowns, yet it still required my physical presence to hold down the fort. I found myself savoring my alone time in the building, when I could process the changes and pray. My days went from working behind the scenes with only a rare meeting to days filled with virtual meetings, both internally and externally with various vendors. Choosing to drive to the office on the weekends not only allowed me more time to work but also gave me space to puzzle through everything going on in the hurricane of changes, allowing me to gain clarity when I desperately needed it. That is when I began what I lovingly call my weekly one-on-ones with God.

Inspired by Ripp's song and by the biblical story of Jericho, I'd walk seven laps around the office, then continue moving through the space in a baseball diamond shape, saying prayers as I stopped at each "base" for a particular prayer topic. Although it may have varied slightly, this is the prayer that became my consistent weekly petition before God as I traced a path around our office during that time:

First Base / First Corner (Psalm 100:4)

Oh God, I lift up your name in this place—
- Elohim–Creator
- El Elyon–The Most High God
- El Olam–Everlasting God
- El Shaddai–God Almighty
- El Roi–The God Who Sees Me
- Yahweh
- Jehovah
- Jehovah-Rohi–The Lord My Shepherd
- Jehovah-Jireh–The Lord Shall Provide
- Jehovah-Rapha–The Lord Who Heals
- Jehovah-Nissi–The Lord Is My Banner
- Jehovah-M'Kaddesh–The Lord Who Sanctifies
- Jehovah-Shalom–The Lord Who Is Peace
- Jehovah-Tsidkenu–The Lord Who Is Righteous
- Jehovah-Shammah–The Lord Who Is There
- Adonai–Lord Master
- Abba–Faithful Father
- My Healer
- My Maker
- My Shield and Great Reward
- Bondage Breaker
- The Great I Am
- Rock of Ages
- Strong Tower
- Alpha and Omega
- Holy Spirit

- *Messiah*
- *Yeshua*
- *Lion of Judah*
- *Lamb of God*
- *Prince of Peace*
- *Mighty God*
- *Everlasting Savior*
- *Jesus*

You are:
- *The Lord above all lords*
- *The King above all kings*
- *The Prince above all princes*
- *The President above all presidents*
- *The Legislature above all legislatures*
- *The Judge above all judges*
- *You are holy and righteous*
- *You are mighty and powerful and strong*
- *You are omniscient, omnipresent, and omnipotent*
- *And yet, You are kind and patient, gracious and generous, and good*
- *You are beautiful and marvelous*
- *You are so worthy to sit upon the throne*
- *So worthy to receive all my praise*

I thank You for Your lovingkindness toward us—for calling us ambassadors and entrusting us with Your name to do good things on Your behalf. You said that what we bind on Earth is bound in heaven, and what we loose on Earth is loosed in heaven.

So in your name, I cast out all division, all discouragement, all depression, all disease, all doubts, and all distractions. I call forth

Your perfect love that casts out all fear, Your peace that passes all understanding to guard our hearts and minds, and the joy of the Lord that is our strength.

Lord, I invite You into this place and ask You to be present with us here. Fill this suite from one end to the other. Fill this building from the top to the bottom, from the sky above to the ground below, out through the courtyard and other buildings, out through the parking lot, the vehicles, and the other businesses on this property.

Please bless the property owners and investors.

Bless the management company and management team.

Bless the engineering team.

Bless the security team.

Bless the janitorial team.

Bless the deli owners and workers.

And pour out that blessing to their families and extended families and everyone they touch.

Please bless us as tenants as we enjoy this beautiful, nice space.

Fill these buildings with good tenants.

Please watch over and protect us here.

In Jesus's precious name, Yeshua Hamashiach.

Second Base / Conference Room Corner (Luke 6:38)

Thank You, God, for this conference room that represents the leadership of the company. Let it be a place of gracious generosity as we host guests and team members.

Please fill it with the fruit of the Spirit: love, joy, peace, forbearance, kindness, goodness, faithfulness, gentleness, and self-control. Give us a love for one another, that we would help and encourage each other.

Help us to have creativity and fresh ideas, along with the skills, strength, and endurance to do the work.

I walk in humility, meekness, and repentance before You. Let repentance and revival begin in this place and flow out to the city, metroplex, counties, state, each and every one of the United States, and out to the rest of the world.

I take all the limits off of You, God, and surrender to what You will do and how You will do it. Increase our capacity to receive so You can increase our capacity to give. Please start pouring out blessings and don't stop, so that it flows from the top leaders of the company down to each and every one of the least of us. Let everybody, even those at the bottom, feel so valued, appreciated, and loved.

Third Base / Third Corner (Numbers 6:24–26)

Lord, pour out Your Shalom over us—nothing missing, nothing broken.

Bless our investors, our board of directors, our executive team, our managers, and workers. Also bless all of our clients and all of our vendors. Let these blessings overflow to their families, extended families, and everyone they touch.

Pour out Your peace, protection, healing, comfort, provision, restoration, and reconciliation. For those who need healing, please heal them. For those who are grieving, please surround them with Your love, cover them with your wings, and comfort them. Provide for those who need provision and restoration.

I thank You that You go before us, behind us, and beside us—and that Your banner over us is love.

Only a couple months later, the company began a series of acquisitions and mergers that left me juggling crushing demands, an hour-long commute, and twenty-four-seven stress. Layering the pandemic on top of that, and its impact on cybersecurity during the time, I was having to learn on my feet and respond to constant challenges like never before.

I told myself I could manage the twelve- to fourteen-hour days for a couple years if I had to, thinking it was just a temporary push during my learning curve while I got established. But every time a respite came into view, we would acquire another company, and the crush would begin again. I could have summited one mountain, but it turned out I was being asked to traverse a whole range of them!

On top of all this, I was still playing a crucial role at the company's emotional and missional heart, leading the Pay It Forward program and offering an ear and a helping hand to anyone who needed it. I missed having the ability to simply accomplish a goal, take a breath, and coast for a while. Heck, I missed being able to breathe at all.

When listening to a John C. Maxwell podcast during that time, this memorable quote completely changed my paradigm and perspective: "Hard doesn't prepare you for easy. Hard prepares you for harder."[3]

It felt like I'd been dropped into an ocean without a life raft. I spent so much time on my knees, telling God I was drowning, only to hear His response: "My child, I'm the God who walks on water. I won't let you drown."

The thing about being dropped in the ocean like that... you wind up becoming a strong swimmer fast. That didn't make the process any less painful.

The near-tragedies and losses. The suffocating stress. The pandemic.

When it rains, it pours; when you enter the cocoon, everything dissolves.

And all of this, it turned out, was just the beginning.

---

3. John Maxwell, "High Road Leadership," Maxwell Leadership Podcast, May 8, 2024.

CHAPTER 9

Dissolving: The Health Crisis That Changed Everything

IT WAS AUGUST of 2022, and I woke up in the middle of the night in excruciating pain.

Have you experienced physical pain so intense it immediately jolts you from sleep and violently wreaks nauseous havoc on you? As the experience recedes into memory, the intensity ebbs from physical pain to a faint memory—and thank God for that. In the moment, though, it feels like it will never, ever end. There's not much like it to teach you total dependence on your Maker, not much else that makes you blindingly aware that your only hope is the miracle-maker of all miracle-makers. You come out of it softened and changed, your perspective forever altered. Not that I'd recommend it for kicks and giggles, of course.

After the years of fertility treatments, I had stubbornly decided on no more optional surgeries. I was so tired of unfruitful tests and treatments. I had been neglecting my health for years. During the time my uncle was in the hospital, I spent almost all of my hours sitting down. This was compounded as my grandmother's health declined and I spent nights with her in the independent living facility, when we hoped that the surgery she'd had to repair her spine would lead her back toward finishing life in good health. But as I sat up with her, sleeping only lightly, trying to make sure she had no falls during the night, I became all the more sedentary. I was no longer merely a couch potato—I had sprouted roots and leaves, like a fully grown potato plant.

Then my overwhelming mountain of work just compounded the time I spent narrowly focused on the mental realm, to the detriment of my body. Although I was vaguely aware of increasing symptoms, it felt like work was more urgent and higher priority than anything else, my body's needs included. I thought that the foundational business systems being put into place would provide a pause when I could turn my attention toward myself and go get a checkup. I was buried deep in one of my most complicated cloud migration projects when the wake-up call finally came, and I certainly never would have expected it to be such a severe one.

The culprit of my agony was a strangulated hernia, as purple as a grape Jolly Rancher and as big as a tennis ball, with a twelve-pound tumor looming right beneath it. Realizing that emergency surgery would be needed if my intestines were involved in the wild tangle my innards had formed around that brisket-sized intruder, I was finally convinced to head to the emergency room. My husband went with me, and he was such a comfort as they gave me morphine to dull the pain. He gently reassured me through the tears that surfaced as I realized I would need surgery. That was the last thing I wanted to do.

During the years of fertility struggles, my first surgery to remove tumors had been beyond intense. Once, as I was recovering in the hospital afterwards, I turned over and the bed began to fill with blood, prompting the nurses to question whether I would require a return to the operating room. My body turned a deep, dark purplish black from right under my chest down to my knees. My legs and ankles swelled to the point that they looked more elephantine than human. I remember my younger sister telling me it looked like I'd been hit by a car. When

I clarified, "Like I was in a car crash?" she doubled down: "No, like you weren't in a car at all, and a car just hit you full force!" The memory of that recovery experience left me with a deep dread of surgery.

But praise God, Psalm 91 came to mind as I panicked in that emergency room and brought me the peace that passes all understanding, a peace that only God can provide.

The emergency room surgeon came in later, reviewing my iodine contrast CAT scan, to talk about the hernia. We both knew that the hernia, though it needed to be fixed, was not the real problem. The true concern was the presence of the giant tumors sitting right behind it. Given the gravity of the situation, he wanted me to see one of the best oncologist surgeons in the area. Though he didn't think the tumors were cancerous, I would need someone with years of experience in complicated tumor removal to perform my risky surgery. I needed to address the threat quickly, but he assured me I would be okay for the week it took to make it to the next appointment.

I remember that one of the first things the new surgeon said, when I met him a week later, was that my situation represented a "trophy" (as I could safely boast to having the largest tumors he had ever seen). But I certainly didn't feel like I had won any prizes.

Knowing that I didn't have enough time before the surgery to visit my sisters in person, who were spread out all over the country, I could only call and say that I love them and ask them to pray. Aside from my husband, both our parents, my sisters, and my husband's sisters, I told almost no one the full story. And very few of those who did know really understood the true nature of the situation: the fact that my life was hanging in the balance. Sometimes, when you are praying for a miracle of that magnitude, it's wise to keep your circle of prayer warriors small and close.

Because my life truly was hanging in the balance. This was a surgery that I wouldn't have survived if it had been undertaken in an emergency setting, apparently. As the surgeon explained, he would normally be lining up compatible blood donations for me in case there was a need for a transfusion, but that wouldn't be the case for me. The fibroid tumors at the root of the problem were sitting directly on top of my blood supply. This meant that only a well-planned, highly complex surgery would do the trick, and even then, if the surgeon wasn't able to get in and out as quickly as intended, I would bleed out too quickly for them to save me, even with blood on hand. He counseled me through pain management in the meantime and let me know I'd likely have no belly button left to speak of if I did survive the surgery. (Later, when he came to check on me in the hospital room after surgery, he said, "I was able to save your belly button after all, but I'm not sure I put it back in the right place"—in that deadpan tone that only a surgeon can pull off. I'm not sure I responded with my usual laughter at the time, because the pain was so intense that it felt like a sword was thrust into my wounds and like the pressure of a mountain was sitting on my spine. It was far more intense and excruciating than my prior surgeries.)

But I'm jumping ahead. During that first appointment, the surgeon sent me to the front desk to set a date on the calendar for one week later. One week before I'd have a mask placed over my face, sink into dreamless sleep, and either wake up cured or not wake up at all.

When have you been forced to accept that you have no control at all—not one iota—and that your very life is in God's hands? Whether you've been through a near-death experience yourself or have been reminded of your own mortality in other ways, there is nothing quite like letting the reality of it all sink in for encouraging dependence on the One who gave us life, and the One who embraces us after death.

It was all too much of a shock to process, at first. I mean, we've all seen the bittersweet movies about people taking the world by storm after a terminal diagnosis, usually with the tagline, "What would YOU do if you had just days to live?" or something like that. In my case, as my mind turned to everything on my personal and professional to-do list, as well as all the people I wanted to see in person and hug, I realized there was no need to write out a bucket list. There was simply not enough time to do any of those things. So, I laid them all down, surrendering everything to the God who held my life in His hands. When you come face-to-face with the complete end of yourself, it allows you to let go of petty things in a way that truly transforms you and sets you free.

I wasn't certain I would die, but I wasn't certain I would live, either. Whichever way it went, I had such a tiny window of time to contend with—too short to really do anything in particular with. I didn't know quite what to do. I was deep, deep in the darkness of the cocoon.

In the end, I realized all I could do was let go and trust in the One who made me.

God continued to put Psalm 91 on my heart throughout those two weeks:

> *Whoever dwells in the shelter of the Most High will rest in the*
> *shadow of the Almighty.*
> *I will say of the Lord, "He is my refuge and my fortress,*
> *my God, in whom I trust."*
> *Surely he will save you*
> *from the fowler's snare*
> *and from the deadly pestilence.*
> *He will cover you with his feathers,*
> *and under his wings you will find refuge;*
> *his faithfulness will be your shield and rampart.*
> *You will not fear the terror of night,*
> *nor the arrow that flies by day,*
> *nor the pestilence that stalks in the darkness,*
> *nor the plague that destroys at midday.*
> *A thousand may fall at your side,*
> *ten thousand at your right hand,*
> *but it will not come near you.*

> *You will only observe with your eyes*
> *   and see the punishment of the wicked.*
> *If you say, "The Lord is my refuge,"*
> *   and you make the Most High your dwelling,*
> *no harm will overtake you,*
> *   no disaster will come near your tent.*
> *For he will command his angels concerning you*
> *   to guard you in all your ways;*
> *they will lift you up in their hands,*
> *   so that you will not strike your foot against a stone.*
> *You will tread on the lion and the cobra;*
> *   you will trample the great lion and the serpent.*
> *"Because he loves me," says the Lord, "I will rescue him;*
> *   I will protect him, for he acknowledges my name.*
> *He will call on me, and I will answer him;*
> *   I will be with him in trouble,*
> *   I will deliver him and honor him.*
> *With long life I will satisfy him*
> *   and show him my salvation."*

Those words gave me so much peace—the most peace I'd ever felt in my whole life, in fact. I repeated them again and again in the days leading up to my surgery.

It's odd to think about now, but one of the primary worries that occupied my mind during those two terrifying weeks was concern for the people I worked with, and for my company at large. At the time, we were still just building the ship as we went. When it came to the technology side of things, I was the leader guiding us all through the jungle, slicing out a path for others to follow with a well-worn machete. There were a lot of people counting on me, and many processes hinged on my continued existence, from account access to the management of sensitive information around our mergers and acquisitions.

DISSOLVING: THE HEALTH CRISIS THAT CHANGED EVERYTHING

I didn't want to create a panic, especially since what I had wasn't a death sentence; it was just the possibility of one. An executive had just been hired who I was planning to make my backup for IT vendor account ownership and access, but he wouldn't be onboarded until after my surgery. I didn't want to let him know that if I died, he would need a stack of death certificates in order to regain ownership of all the accounts. If you have never had to do that, you have no idea just the level of pain, time, and paperwork involved.

Although I had passwords saved in a password manager, it was all wrapped with "MFA" (multi-factor authentication), which meant he would have been powerless without my phone. I did let him and my main contact at the Board of Directors know how to access the password manager, just in case. But otherwise, what was I supposed to say to him? "Hey, nice to meet you! I might be dead in two weeks, and we don't really have enough time to make a plan, so... good luck!"

Normally a very private person, my natural instinct was not to tell anyone at work except a few colleagues in my immediate orbit, but the foundational work I had been doing on business systems and processes touched every area of the business. And the leadership I had been doing through Pay It Forward had, at its heart, my desire to pour love, joy, compassion, and kindness into employees first, knowing that would naturally extend to the communities around them.

I'd celebrated babies, grandbabies, nieces, and nephews being born, but I'd also attended so many funerals, sometime multiple at a time, especially during the height of the pandemic. We'd served meals at Union Gospel Mission and repaired houses for Meals on Wheels together as a team. I felt the weight of shock they would feel if I didn't survive and they didn't even know I was having surgery. How could I do that to them?

So, I sucked it up, and sent a company-wide email, basically saying, "Hey world, I'm having a surgery, but it's no big deal, I'll be fine!" in the most cheerful, optimistic, and encouraging tone I could muster up. (It reminded me of my older sister when she was in grade school. Out on the playground, a friend asked where she was going, when she bellowed in a yell that reverberated across the entire space, "I'm going to the bathroom!" Quite an embarrassing situation for a grade schooler, no doubt!)

In the end, I did fib a little bit. I told everyone I was having a hysterectomy and assured them I'd be back in the office after two weeks (instead of the usual recommendation of six to eight weeks of recovery). This choice to keep the situation close to the vest helped me release the outcomes, and my doubts, into God's hands. And in the end, my assurances proved almost prophetic. I was, indeed, back on my feet very quickly.

My time in the cocoon was one of utter, unknowing darkness. I could not see an inch farther than the tip of my nose. I don't know if the mid-metamorphosis goo-creature—not quite caterpillar, not quite butterfly—has any real consciousness of its situation. I imagine it knows nothing at all, and I relate.

During those two weeks, I could not predict with any real certainty whether I would simply succumb in that cramped, dark space, or whether I would emerge changed. All I could do—perhaps something like the goo-creature—was trust the process, let go of control, and step forward in faith.

I pray that as you navigate your own cocoon, you are able to do the same.

CHAPTER 10

Being Remade

BEING IN THE cocoon is so hard. Take a minute, again, to think about the visceral reality of it: The caterpillar actually dissolves itself, and for a time is neither caterpillar nor butterfly, just some muddled-up, in-between, gloopy thing. In our own lives, in our own "cocoon moments," this can feel so confusing, dark, bewildering... yet also so full of promise, excitement, and hope! It truly is an existential struggle. Dramatic transformation is hard, full of resistance, as you begin to exercise new wings that are not yet completely formed, without even hitting the walls of your encapsulation, over and over, again and again. You think you're ready to burst out of the shell, but you will face resistance, and there is no avoiding it or speeding God's timing along. It's the pressure of mountains and depths of the sea that hardens diamonds. It's the pushing at the walls of the cocoon that strengthens your wings for flight.

Needless to say, my surgery was successful. I did not die on that operating table; but my time in the cocoon wasn't over quite yet, either. I had to spend some time flexing my unformed wings, pushing against my own walls, because as the butterfly can teach us, being taken apart and put back together again takes time and patience! Whatever Hollywood may have to say about it, growth is never a quick and instant process—even with the initial, catalyzing jolt of a dramatic near-death experience.

The first two weeks of my recovery were difficult, but in comparison to previous surgeries, I honestly felt pretty amazing. It was truly miraculous (though I certainly don't want to downplay how much having one of the top surgeons in the area contributed to my relatively quick recuperation, along with the transformative help of an abdominal binder during the healing process—such an opposite experience from my first fibroid surgery).

It was only once I returned to work that the physical toll of the surgery really showed up. I went from working long days, twelve or fourteen hours of sheer focus and effort, to being physically spent by 5 p.m. I had previously functioned something like a wild mustang, galloping fast and hard across the wide-open plains without flagging, and now I was moving like a sloth on Benadryl—spending hours sleeping, struggling to eat well, and doing what felt like the bare minimum in extreme slow motion. When I was cleared to drive and decided to return to the office in person, I found I couldn't even get through a light eight-hour day without quietly disappearing midafternoon for a nap on a couch in the unused back office.

Oh, I hated feeling that way—at the mercy of my body and its needs and limitations. I can't count the number of times I chided myself: "What is wrong with you?" I was perpetually behind on my work and under pressure, but I felt physically incapable of moving faster than a crawl. It was painful, not least because it forced me to truly realize how much stock I had come to place in my own professional competence and performance. How much of my self-worth and identity had gotten wrapped into my work? In truth, I could no longer see daylight between the two. I was my work, and finding myself unable to do the job up to my own high standards shattered me.

Thank God, He knows what He's doing. In the midst of my distress, He began to confront me, dredging up deep questions about identity, rest, visibility, and who He truly created me to be. Sometimes it felt like a conversation, and sometimes it felt a bit more like... well, war. At times, in the middle of a workday, I'd be forced to close the office door to reach out to God for some words of wisdom and comfort. One day in prayer, He brought me to this verse from Zechariah: "Do not despise these small beginnings, for the Lord rejoices to see the work begin." That was the moment when the tide began to turn, when I realized I didn't have to carry it all. Slow steps were still progress. Real growth—meaningful change beyond the "daily grind," or attempts to climb the corporate ladder—sometimes hurt. True metamorphosis moved at God's pace, not my own.

When have you been reminded of your utter dependence on God? Have you ever found yourself simply unable to do the things you believe make you you, and fallen back into God's arms and a fresh understanding of what it means to simply be?

It's odd to realize now, but I had been working and pushing so hard for so long, expecting some kind of payoff to come around the bend. Instead, I hit a professional ceiling—a ceiling that, as my friend Drew pointed out when I wept to him in frustration and dejection, turned out to be me. I thought my hard work, sacrifice, and struggle would earn me promotions, and that I was helping my team by breaking my back and being so self-reliant, when really, I was crippling their ability to grow and pushing my own development to the side in the process. I remember one day, leaning against the cabinets with my office door closed, completely at the end of myself: tired, frustrated, ready to quit. Somehow, I stumbled across an episode of the Craig Groschel podcast with Louie Giglio that spoke perfectly to my situation.[4]

When Louie talked about "good quitting," when you release something totally to God and go get some sleep, that idea gave me the

---

4. "Discover Your Leadership Style," The Craig Groschel Podcast, December 21, 2023.

permission to finally let go. Then Craig said something else that was a turning point for me: "Everyone wins when the leader gets better." Because what I had thought was servant leadership was actually neglect. I needed to start investing in myself. It wasn't selfish to do that, but actually something that would benefit everyone around me too.

God was urging me to slow down, to care for myself, to lean into a period of sabbath. He was reminding me that He was in control, and that He was my defender. One day around this time, in the middle of the night, God woke me up, prompting me to buy fencing sport equipment. I had taken a fencing class for a semester in college, but I was woefully out of shape and in no mood to join a class of kids in order to relearn the sport. However, the urging was so strong that I relented and browsed Amazon to find a foil, target, and sport mask and purchased them, wondering all the while how my husband would respond to this craziness. Then I drifted back to sleep.

God has a funky sense of humor sometimes, but eventually I understood the point of that moment. As I stood in my home holding the fencing foil, I realized I would only ever be able to practice offense—without a sparring partner, there was no real way to learn defensive moves. I could almost feel His wink as I had this epiphany: "Exactly, Shelly. You cannot put up your own defense. I'm your defense. Let me be your shield. Don't worry about being rejected and extracted from company leadership. I'm protecting you for your purpose."

My feelings of rejection at the time were complex and overpoweringly real. I had kept so much around my health journey bottled up, unshared with my leadership team. As a consequence, I felt unseen. Then, one day, Hebrews 6:10–12 came up during prayer: "God is not unjust; He will not forget your work and the love you have shown Him." God saw me, and valued me, whether I earned titles and public applause for my hard work… or not. He sees and values you, no matter what, too.

Leadership, He reminded me, was about so much more than formal recognition. Somewhere along the way, I'd not only neglected my own personal and professional growth, but when had I last actively mentored someone, as a true leader should? I began pursuing updated leadership credentials and building a new network, looking for opportunities to give back. I asked God to lead me to places where I could support others.

As an introvert, diving back into the challenges of networking was hard. It wasn't a fear of facing crowds—I could perform, speak, lead small groups. I had done that through church and charity events. But chit-chat over drinks? Terrifying. I had to fight the urge to cling to the nearest fellow introvert, but repetition helped. God kept encouraging me to keep showing up, reminding me that doing so was half the battle. Seeing familiar faces made it easier. I found ways to network "my way," making real friendships instead of just exchanging business cards.

God was working through my identity on so many levels, not just in regard to my professional path and growth as a leader. I joined an online women's Bible study in September 2023, exactly one year after my surgery. The group was started by women who had a jewelry business. When you ordered a necklace from them, they would choose a word to engrave for you, pray over it, and send it to you with a prophetic word. The word they first sent to me was "forerunner," which was totally unexpected—I'm still unpacking the meaning of that title today. As I searched the Bible, always feeling the need to vet prophetic words against Scripture, I found that the only verse that had the word "forerunner" in it was, again, Hebrews 6: the passage that reminded me that God saw and valued me, no matter what.

Connecting with that jewelry business led me to the related Bible study, and that group made such a difference for my spiritual walk and growth.

Through that study, I began collecting more of those necklaces with different words on them—reminders of what God had spoken to me. I would pray over each one, especially during hard weeks. Throughout this time, God would sometimes give me the most strange instructions. Things that you would pray could be done quietly outside the purview of others, because they seemed so crazy. He told me to start wearing the necklaces as I prayed—yes, all of them! I'd put them on in the car before my commute to the office and take them off before anyone could see such ridiculousness. But on the weekends, as I would do my one-on-ones with God, I would wear them, necklaces clinking, feeling more than a tad silly.

Then one Saturday morning, sitting at home as I prepared to head to the office, I had been feeling so convicted about not observing a sabbath. So, I whispered a prayer to God, that I would dedicate that day to whatever He wanted me to do. Unless He redirected me, I would head to the office, but that day was His.

Almost immediately after that prayer, I saw a post on LinkedIn about "telling your story," and heard Him clearly say, "Write a book." My initial puzzled thought was "What?" and then a bit of a smug thought that it would be easy. After all, I had graduated from a college that had such a focus on writing that I had to write a research paper simply for taking a dance class.

Little did I know the depths of what it would entail. A process that would dig into the depths of my soul to bring healing to myself and others and be an integral part of my metamorphosis. He was calling me not only to write a book, but to be visible, be bold, speak up and share my story, take the stage, and move into the spotlight. It was frightening!

Around that same time, God led me back to the story of Jericho. I had never thought before about how the Israelites had to be completely silent for six days before letting out their mighty, wall-tumbling shout. God was telling me to "maintain radio silence." As an introvert, you would think that would be an easy task, but it proved to be harder than I could ever imagine. Not only was it a struggle to avoid speaking about things with people, but I was also having to silence all my own negative internal dialogue. I had been completely unaware of the things my mind was saying to me, or repeating what others said about me, that did not align with God's goodness.

At the same time, in the paradoxical way that God sometimes works, He was also telling me to "speak boldly." My brain struggled to understand why God would give me two puzzle pieces that seemed to completely contradict one another. However, over time, I realized God was taking me to a higher level of discernment—teaching me to recognize when to speak up and when to remain quiet.

Then one day, God told me, in the way He speaks into your spirit, "Be visible. I didn't make you to be invisible."

At first, I politely said, "No thank you, God. Don't you know that I'm an introvert?!"

To which He replied, "I told you to be visible."

And we began to go round and round, like a parent arguing with an obstinate toddler: "No thank you, I don't want to be visible,"

"Be visible."

"No thank you," and so on.

Until finally, in complete exasperation, I replied: "I can't be visible. I might die!"

Before the words were even fully uttered, I was completely stunned and surprised that I would say something so ridiculous. Where in the world did that come from? I couldn't imagine what would cause such a visceral, fearful reaction to such a simple request from God. As only God can do, He was revealing a very dysfunctional survival mechanism that had begun in my childhood. I didn't realize that hiding behind my quiet, introverted personality was a huge weed that needed to be plucked out.

"I didn't make you to be invisible," He repeated quietly. "I made you to be visible, to shine."

During that nightmarish period of my stepfather's abuse, hiding had come to feel like home. Invisibility, God helped me finally realize, was something I still equated with safety, in my heart of hearts. By consequence, God's calling to step into a place of heightened visibility scared me as much as if He were telling me to step out onto a battlefield with no armor, no weapons, in plain view and within firing range of countless armed enemies.

I wonder if you can identify any of those behavior patterns or protective mechanisms that linger in your own life today—scars of wounds that no longer serve a purpose. I pray God guides you to confront them as He guided me: gently, patiently, with a bit of teasing and an affectionate reprimand or two.

Then there was another time while I was driving, having some sort of internal dialogue or prayer. God's message in that moment was so shocking that it caused me to completely forget exactly what I was saying, other than the fact that I was talking to myself about how easygoing I was.

God stopped me and immediately said, "No, you are not easygoing! You are passionate, emotional, driven, ambitious, and intense."

To which I replied, again like an obstinate toddler, "I am too easygoing!"

God's response was, "No, you are not! And I should know, because I'm the One who made you."

"But I'm not a jerk," I questioned Him tentatively, "or somebody who's flighty, like a hippie or something."

"Of course you aren't," He said, "because you are also extremely patient, extremely kind, compassionate, sensitive, and empathetic. And these opposites balance things out. You're not broken, and I didn't make a mistake. I made you the way you are on purpose!"

He reminded me: Compassion, sensitivity, and tenderness are not weaknesses. It's sensitivity that allows a brain surgeon to operate or a painter to create something divine.

"Your tears are your strength," He said. "Compassion moves you, as it moves Me, like a mother grizzly is moved when her cub cries."

The parts of me I'd long hidden away or feared make me who I am and deserve a place in my story.

Have you ever argued with God? Felt like a stubborn child, insisting you know more than the Maker of the universe? I'm sure we've all been there at some point and learned the hard way how very foolish it is. I wonder where He has led, and continues to lead you, through both the mature, reflective prayers and the emotional, toddler-ish dialogues.

One day, God took me to the story of Esther. Queen Vashti had refused to show herself and demonstrate the King's glory, a twisted kind of humility that, really, stemmed from pride. God told me, "You can be humble and still shine. Just give Me the glory."

The time had come to step up and speak. The time had come to write this book.

At first, I thought maybe the book should just be something business-related, perhaps reflecting on my surgery and how the experience taught me the necessity of having a disaster recovery plan. But as I got into it, what flowed out was a memoir that was about so much more than that.

This book became the story of how God has formed me, broken me down, and reformed me. It has been a huge part of my continuing journey through that continuing reweaving. It has been one of the biggest pieces contributing to the final, triumphant step: breaking out of the cocoon.

PART 4
Butterfly
(AND THE JOURNEY AHEAD)

CHAPTER 11

The Messy Process of Breaking Free

MERGING FROM A cocoon is not a graceful undertaking. I used to imagine a butterfly's emergence from its chrysalis as a kind of beautiful, linear moment—the tiny shell splitting open to reveal an iridescent creature that immediately leaps out and soars away into a sun-drenched sky. But as I've struggled through my own moment of emergence, I've been surprised by how fragile I still feel. My wings, though new, are still damp. My body aches from the struggle it took to break through. And my spirit, freshly rewoven by the grace of God, is still learning how to fly.

My near-death experience forced me into a time of rest and reflection that I would probably never have chosen on my own. That time of stillness—and the professional disappointments and disillusionment that followed—dismantled the architecture of my life. It broke apart the scaffolding I had built around my identity: success, performance, productivity, control. I found myself in a sacred pause, a cocoon not of my choosing, but one designed by God to slow me down, strip me bare, and then carefully reassemble me.

Following God's call, I stepped into increased visibility, and I accepted the task He gave me: the task of writing this book. I didn't know then that it was a mechanism God would use to begin recreating my identity—a period built not on what I could do, but on who I was becoming. I thought I had buried certain parts of myself for good: my creativity, the love for design I inherited from my mom, my desire to give thoughtful, beautiful gifts. I'd long ago given those passions a funeral, thinking they didn't belong in the serious, strategic world of leadership and IT. And yet, during this in-between season, they began to resurrect.

God had been sowing the seeds for this already, in small ways I hadn't recognized. When I first moved into the IT director position, I also inherited the responsibility of helping to maintain and be a point of contact for our office suite. We'd moved in before the company was divested from the larger corporation and had not been allowed any budget for new office furniture or decor at the time. As a result, the empty gray walls and gray cubicles, devoid of any life, left me feeling so depressed. I decided that if I was going to spend long hours there, I wanted it to be a space filled with beauty, joy, life, and laughter.

When people returned after COVID, I convinced them to give me a $4,000 budget for updates (though almost half of that money was spent getting 1-800-GOT-JUNK to haul off all the old mismatched bookshelves, file cabinets, outdated desk accessories, and chairs so broken that I feared someone would sit in them, fall or collapse, and break their neck). People would ask why in the world I was spending my free time doing interior design work and assembling chairs and cabinets, helping paint the old conference table to an updated finish, even bringing in some decor that I had purchased for staging my house when I had it on the market, to fill in for the budget shortcomings. After all, I was the IT director, with a mountain of business systems to build! To which I would reply that I needed a creative outlet, and it was reducing my stress. Beyond that, it was so rewarding when, during the peak tax season, the people who returned to the office told me how much better things looked and that it felt so good to be there.

Then we acquired a new company that did work around SALT (Sales and Local Tax). The sales and marketing teams mentioned wanting to do some campaigns playing around with that acronym, and for some reason, I lit up like a Labrador retriever who had just been given a new tennis ball. Smoked sea salt is one of my absolute favorite things of all time. I volunteered to design a gift box to use as sales and marketing were working out the target list of prospects for the campaign.

I busily arranged for a local spice and tea shop to custom label a set of salts, with other things included to round out the kit of gift items. Then, because I had been working so heavily in our CRM, I designed landing pages, email-to-case flows, and a QR code printed on a customized mailing box. It was looking amazing, when suddenly someone said, "Wait, why are you doing all that? You're the IT director! Give that to marketing!"

Feeling so completely deflated, I spent some time afterward pondering why in the world I went after that project with such zeal and passion. Maybe I just… really loved sea salt, so, so much?

Then, in the middle of the night, I woke up to this revelation from God: "Don't you remember? Growing up in your mom's business, they did the gifts for the 1996 Summer Olympics in Atlanta. And before that, The Vineyard did the gift-with-purchase for Paloma Picasso perfume. They even brought in a night shift to make all the red frames for that project. Your talent for making gifts like that is practically baked into your DNA. You've always loved and been talented at creating gifts, just like your mother was in her business."

I was finally starting to realize that these little pieces of me weren't distractions from my purpose but clues to it.

God was pulling out of storage all the old, forgotten, dust-covered parts of my story and weaving them back into something new. And while it felt confusing at times, it also felt like coming home to myself.

The thing about finally breaking out of the cocoon, after that long, dark period of reweaving, is that the journey doesn't end there. Many butterflies migrate across oceans and continents during the brief span of their lives. All butterflies go somewhere… at least, once their wings dry and once they learn to fly.

Painted lady butterflies are small, seemingly delicate creatures, but a tattered few were once confirmed to have flown over 2,600 miles across the Atlantic Ocean. Scientists were stunned. They must have looked so out of place when they landed, impossibly, on that beach in French Guiana. As if simply breaking out of the cocoon wasn't difficult enough! The hard part was far from over, and they embarked on a journey even the hardiest of hobbits might have marveled at.

We spend our lives being broken down, shedding, letting go, and being rewoven by God's grace, but the real work doesn't simply end. When the disguise has been peeled back and you stand vulnerable in the light, you have to learn to live unmasked. I had so many layers of camouflage built up, like Sherlock Holmes hiding inside a chair suit. I had learned to disappear, thinking it was the safest way to move through the world. But as God beckoned me into this new period of visibility, He showed me that simply existing as myself, being seen as who I truly was, wasn't a threat anymore. Not when He was my protector. Not when my identity was hidden in Him.

I had worn masks so long, I forgot what my face looked like, but God never did. In His gentle, persistent way, He kept tugging at the masks. He kept whispering, "Come out. I've made you for more than this!"

The plan I had so carefully laid out for my life turned out to be far too small. God's plan was wider, deeper, and more beautiful than I could've ever designed. It didn't always look logical, and it didn't always feel safe. But it was good.

And so here I am! Wings still wet, not yet soaring, but not in the cocoon either. I don't know exactly what's next, but I know who's leading, and that's enough.

The trees that require fire to reproduce remind us—sometimes destruction is the very condition for new life. What you survive becomes what qualifies you to lead. The ashes of your experience become fertilizer for someone else's growth. You can't walk the path for others, but you can light it with the lessons you've learned.

And so, if you're reading this—still in your cocoon or just emerging—I want to encourage you! The struggle to break free isn't the end. It's just the beginning. What has brought you to the end of yourself has actually brought you to the beginning of something bigger than you could imagine.

Gather up all your pieces—the beautiful, the broken, the buried—and offer them back to the One who can make something new. Watch what He does with them.

CHAPTER 12

Looking Back, Moving Forward

AS YOU CLOSE out your reading of this book, I want to turn the spotlight on you.

My story has followed the pattern of a butterfly's life: its hatching and nourishing, its growth and molting, its muddled time in the cocoon, its messy emergence, its slowly spreading wings. I wonder whether, in looking back over your own life, you might see a similar pattern.

To that end, I'd encourage you to set aside some quiet time to look over your life. Use the questions below, drawn from my own story, to seek out God's work in yours. Pray as you go, write down your thoughts along the way, and really let it settle in. My hope is that you will be encouraged in your own falling apart and coming together, that you will see the patterns and moments of light even in your darkest memories.

(A note before you dive in: I don't know where you are in your journey! Maybe you aren't past your cocoon moment yet. Maybe you aren't even approaching it. These questions follow the complete span of that journey, but if you don't feel you've reached a certain stage yet, don't try to force it. Simply reflect on the stages and questions that feel helpful and ring true.)

Childhood: Hatching & Early Growth

1. What were the first forms of nourishment and protection you received? How did they shape your sense of safety and worth?

2. How did your family's stories and temperaments mold your earliest identity?

3. What traits or tendencies showed up in your youngest self most prominently—and do they still appear and define you somehow today?

4. What memories from childhood stand out most clearly? Are there gaps or haze around others?

5. Who was consistently present for you? What did their presence offer?

6. How did you respond to fear or challenge as a child—and how does that echo in your responses now? Are you holding on to any self-protective mechanisms learned from that time?

7. What things were you given as a child, and what things were stripped away?

8. Was there a moment of deep darkness in childhood? How did it leave its mark?

9. Where, if at all, did you feel God's presence in your early years?

Young Adulthood: Growth & Molting

1. When did you begin to claim your identity beyond the markers of your upbringing?

2. Have you experienced "molting" seasons, when an old identity or role was shed for growth to occur?

3. How has your understanding of your purpose evolved? What dreams have endured? Which have shifted or been laid down?

4. Have you ever lost your sense of who you are—through grief, change, or failure? How did you begin to rebuild?

5. What "crossroad" moments have shaped your path: choices about career, calling, relationships?

6. Have you ever tied your identity to achievement, success, or roles? How did that play out?

7. How have your passions, talents, and interests shaped your story, and do you still see those threads today?

8. Where do you see God's fingerprints in moments that once felt random or painful?

9. What relationships broke or disappointed you? What did they teach you?

10. Are there places in your heart where hope has been deferred, and protection built up around the wound? What might healing look like there?

Transformation: The Cocoon

1. What was your "cocoon" moment: your season of collapse, stillness, or undoing?

2. Did you feel God with you in that place? If not then, can you see signs of His presence now?

3. When were you brought to the edge of your own control and forced to rely fully on grace?

4. What foundations were quietly laid in that darkness, provisions that only became clear in hindsight?

5. How were you changed by the stillness, the silence, or the suffering?

Emerging: New Life & Migration

1. What has emerged from your season of transformation? New truths, new direction, new peace?

2. How are you beginning to fly, and what is the "migration" you feel drawn to now?

3. What former pieces of your story are now integrated into who you've become?

4. Where are you still learning to trust your wings?

5. Where is God calling you next, and what would it take to say yes?

As we come to the end of this journey—mine on these pages, and yours through your reflection—let's pause together a moment in prayer.

God of all beginnings, thank You for the mystery and mercy of transformation. Thank You for being present in the hatching, in the stretching, in the dark, hidden cocoon, and in the moments when new wings tremble toward the sky.

Lord, I lift up every reader who has walked through these pages. You know their story more intimately than they ever could. You were there at their first breath, and You are already waiting at their next becoming.

Wherever they are in their own journey through metamorphosis, I ask that You meet them there. Open their eyes to the patterns of grace in their past. Speak gently to the broken places. Stir courage where fear once lived. Help them see how even the broken pieces are being woven into beauty.

May the truth of Your Word in 2 Corinthians 5:17 take root in their spirit: "If anyone is in Christ, they are a new creation. The old has gone, the new has come."

We are new creations, born of Your Spirit, marked by Your love, destined for Your purposes.

In Jesus' name,
Amen.

Notes

Notes

Acknowledgments

I WOULD LIKE TO thank Alex Demczak, Will Severns, Hallie Knox, Jessica Burdg, Anton Khodakovsky, Brittany Becker, Becca Blackburn, Chloie Benton, Annika Campbell, and the entire team at Streamline Books. This book would not have been possible without the amazing contributions you made. You are all awesome, and it is so exciting to see not only what you did for me, but what you continue to do for all the other authors and speakers in the community.

And to all the other authors and speakers in the Streamline community: You have been such an inspiration to me. We are truly stronger and more resilient together.

To Jason McCann, thank you for being one of the sparks that brought me back to life. I am so honored to be part of your legacy—a banyan tree.

Thank you to Jeff Lamb, who introduced the works of Patrick Lencioni to Jason, which led me to the six types of working genius. I gained valuable insights into my personality, the work that energizes me, and tendencies that need to be tempered, which has deeply strengthened my leadership abilities.

And I also want to thank my health coach at Living Well Dallas, Celia Naples, who encouraged me to keep going and recognized the way that writing this book made a difference to my healing and overall well-being.

And to my executive coach, Bill Tingle, your support and practical advice is continuing to expand me in all the thirteen areas of life, not only to become a stronger leader, but a well-rounded person of excellence overall, both at work and home.

To Anne Jackson and Katelyn Alexander at The Crowning Jewels, thank you for helping me untangle my identity, so it could again be firmly planted in the knowledge of who I am in Christ. And for the beautiful jewelry and prophetic words that spoke such life into me.

I am so appreciative of Jonathan Harkless and Vip Vipperman, who created and continue to lead the Better Things prayer breakfast, for providing not only a place to give and receive prayer but also bringing in amazing speakers to inspire us. Thank you to Stephanie Adams for inviting me and so many others to join. This community has been such a great support to me, and it became the safe place I needed as I rebuilt my confidence.

So grateful to Joe Fang (joefangheadshots.com) for the photography that captured my personality, allowing me to exude the joy, optimism, and warmth that I hope is reflected in this book.

There are so many others who have played an integral part in my story that I could write an entire book trying to list all the people and things they did to help. Please know that even if you haven't been named here specifically, that you are so valued, loved, and appreciated.

About the Author

SHELLY REXROAT is a visionary designer, technologist, author, and speaker who leads with curiosity, conviction, and compassion. Over nearly three decades, she built transformative and future-forward solutions in a specialized B2B tax firm—often years ahead of their time. Her insatiable love of learning and deep sense of purpose continue to guide her into writing, speaking, and leadership in new industries.

Raised by an entrepreneurial mother who built a home goods business from the ground up, Shelly's world was filled with texture, beauty, and grit. That foundation, paired with her multifaceted blend of strengths, fuels her leadership style—one that is driven by values, deeply attuned to people, elevated by her gift for seeing the unique strengths in others, and committed to seeing people thrive. She helps people and organizations create bold vision and move forward with confidence, igniting momentum with laughter, encouragement, insight, and the belief that meaningful change is always within reach.

Equal parts dreamer and doer, with a brain for big ideas and a heart driven by purpose, she brings deep curiosity and joyful energy. She is wired to make complexity understandable with a gift for making complicated things beautifully clear. Whether designing future-ready technology or physical products and spaces, entertaining with Southern hospitality, or drawing from her background in psychology and a lifelong love of fashion, design, and architecture, she leads with a rare blend of logic, creativity, and imagination.

She's as comfortable designing enterprise systems or crafting organizational and cost efficiencies as she is writing poetry or mentoring future leaders. When speaking on stage, advising executives, or navigating life's hard seasons, she brings thoughtful insight, relational warmth, and bold optimism to everything she does. Her life is a mosaic of musicals, tech strategy sessions, student exchange adventures, deep conversations, and resilient reinvention. Her journey—from performing arts to Senate intern, from software developer to strategic advisor—is a testament to a curious mind and a deep desire to advocate for what matters.

She creates with intention, instructs with heart, and builds with design-first clarity. Her writing, leadership, and speaking all share one mission: to make the world a better, more human, and more beautiful place—through insight, creativity, and connection.

She currently lives in Texas with her husband, Donnie, a physical therapist and award-winning cheerleading coach.

www.ingramcontent.com/pod-product-compliance
Lightning Source LLC
Chambersburg PA
CBHW070241010526
44107CB00041B/1480/J